Mr Lupe Class of '54'
Thanks for
always being there
for us

Blessing
Ann Jasper

and, YES I did hand in
my homework

BEYOND AMAZING GRACE

John Newton

BEYOND AMAZING GRACE

Timeless pastoral wisdom from the letters,
sermons and hymns of John Newton

Compiled and edited by
J. Todd Murray

 EVANGELICAL PRESS

EVANGELICAL PRESS
Faverdale North, Darlington, DL3 0PH, England

e-mail: sales@evangelicalpress.org

Evangelical Press USA
P. O. Box 825, Webster, New York 14580, USA

e-mail: usa.sales@evangelicalpress.org

web: http://www.evangelicalpress.org

First published 2007

British Library Cataloguing in Publication Data available

ISBN 13 978 0 85234 653 2   ISBN 0 85234 653 0

Unless otherwise indicated, Scripture quotations in this publication (other than those which form an integral part of a longer quotation) are taken from the NEW AMERICAN STANDARD BIBLE®, Copyright © 1960, 1962, 1963, 1968, 1971, 1972, 1973, 1975, 1977, 1995 by The Lockman Foundation. Used by permission.

Scripture quotations marked 'AV' are taken from the Authorized / King James Version

Printed and bound in Great Britain by Biddles Ltd, King's Lynn, Norfolk

To my precious wife, Tandy

If Newton's love for Mary was idolatrous,
then I am doubly guilty.
You are indeed
'my pleasing companion,
my most affectionate friend,
and my most judicious counsellor'.

'Marriage … affords the nearest approach to happiness … that can
be attained to in this uncertain world.'
(John Newton, from the preface to *Letters to a Wife*)

Contents

	Page
Preface	11
Acknowledgements	13
Introduction — a biographical sketch of John Newton	15

1. So great salvation

Newton's own conversion

This rebel made a son	23
Through many dangers	26
No more resolves	30

The love of God

His boundless patience	36
Plenteous redemption	39
Wakened by the force of love	44

Sovereign grace

A heart of stone	49
Grace reigns	53
But now I see	57
Essentials in Christianity	60

Assurance of salvation

Do I love the Lord?	64
A solid, permanent assurance	67
On his promise I rely	73
The enemies of assurance	78

2. Growing in holiness

Progressive sanctification
    Grace in the blade   83
    Grace in the ear   86
    Grace in the full corn   92

Battling remaining sin
    I would not ... yet I   96
    What a contradiction!   99
    Defining a Christian   103
    A leprous house   106
    Blemished biographies   110
    Satan's mirror   113
    Holy ambition   116
    On modesty   120
    A pervasive faith   123
    Counselling yourself   126
    Real humility   130

God's purposes in trials
    These inward trials   135
    Good fruit from a bitter root   137
    Tried like Abraham   141

3. Spiritual disciplines

Reading and meditation
    A Bible Christian   147
    On reading the Scriptures   153
    Using the law 'lawfully'   156
    Listening to sermons   159
    The Word as a sword   165

Prayer
    Weakness in prayer   169
    Power in prayer   172
    Improving your public prayers   175

Personal worship
    My soul, what can you give?   180

Songs angels cannot sing   183
The song of the redeemed   186
To whom shall we go?   190
Amazing grace   193

Family worship
Spiritual leadership of children   200
Children away from home   204
Spiritual leadership of wives   209

Evangelism
Ambassadors for Christ   213
Christ, the great divider   217
The cure for unbelief   221

Knowing the will of God
Divine guidance   226

4. Pastoral ministry

The minister and his work
A pastor's joys and griefs   235
Advice to fellow ministers   241

Nuggets of wisdom
A selection of conversational gems   250

5. Hope beyond the grave

On the loss of a loved one
What a change is before me!   255
Yet I will rejoice in the Lord   259

Newton's last days
Waiting for the post   273

Bibliography   279
Notes   281

Illustrations

John Newton   Frontispiece
Facsimile of a page from the *Olney Hymns*   22
William Cowper   67
William Bull   69
The Old Vicarage, Olney, from the churchyard   82
Bedlam   142
Olney parish church   146
Newton's pulpit at St Mary Woolnoth   161
The Old Vicarage, Olney   201
An early draft of a hymn in Newton's handwriting   234
Thomas Scott   242
John Newton's tomb at Olney   254
Commemorative plaque at St Mary Woolnoth   276

Illustrations on the following pages are reproduced by permission of the copyholders:

Page 2, CMS for permission to reproduce the portrait
Pages 2, 69: 242, photos courtesy of The John Newton Project www.johnnewton.org
Pages 82, 146, 161, 201, 254, 276, Graham Hind
Page 234, Lambeth Palace Library

Preface

Several years ago, I came across the lyrics to a hymn by John Newton that I had never heard before, entitled 'Prayers Answered by Crosses', which I found to be infinitely more profound than 'Amazing Grace'. It was the intense impact made on me by this hymn that ultimately led to the compiling of this book. As a Christian, this hymn comforted me that I was not alone in my struggle to understand and trust the purposes of God in my trials. As a songwriter, I was compelled to try to create music that would enhance this penetrating text. As a pastor, I was curious to learn more about the life and works of a fellow minister who wrote such breathtakingly moving words.

My curiosity turned to fascination in the summer of 1998, when my family and I had the first opportunity to visit the little town of Olney, where Newton ministered for sixteen years. There I saw the parsonage where Newton lived and studied, the church and the pulpit in which he preached, the lovely River Ouse along the banks of which he walked with William Cowper, and the cemetery in which he and his wife Mary are buried. In the gift shop of the Cowper and Newton Museum, my wife encouraged me to purchase a facsimile copy of the first edition (1779) of the *Olney Hymnal*, the most important souvenir I have ever bought! That little green volume and *The Works of John Newton*, together with a stream of biographies, both old and new, have been my constant companions ever since. My fascination has turned to love — not that of a scholar, but rather the grateful admiration of one who has been helped and strengthened by Newton's letters and sermons, as well as by his hymns. Through the written page, Newton has become a mentor and a friend, a companion in my own maturing as a believer and a pastor.

I know that not everyone will have the time or interest to peruse the thousands of pages which make up Newton's works, so in this book I have attempted to share his writings with a wider audience. In order to make these more accessible to a modern reader, the spelling and punctuation have been lightly edited, to bring them more in line with current practice, and a number of explanatory comments have been included in brackets, where words have changed their meaning or largely gone out of use since Newton's day.

While many preachers within the eighteenth-century Evangelical movement, including Newton himself, addressed the weighty and essential doctrine of justification by faith, I know of no other writer from this period of church history who offered so much clear teaching on *sanctification* as he did. His candid and humble insights into every believer's battle with remaining sin and his teaching on trusting God during affliction and suffering are certainly the hallmarks of his ministry. I pray that your joy in your walk with God will be increased, as mine has been, as you read and listen to the kind wisdom of this often overlooked man of God.

J. Todd Murray

Acknowledgements

I am deeply indebted to the following people for their part in bringing this book to fruition:

My fellow elders and congregation of The Bible Church of Little Rock for giving me a sabbatical from pastoral ministry in order to write this book.

Jean Blair, Mary Kate Arrington, Rev. Glynn and Ruth Ann Hill, Dr David and Nina Baker for faithfully praying during the writing of this book.

Wanda Gerke for proofreading and locating excerpts (and actually liking it!)

Ramona Gray, my mother-in-law, for making the trip to Olney possible and for the use of your home as a writer's retreat.

Dr and Mrs John Wallace for allowing me to tour the Old Vicarage in Olney.

Marylynn Rouse for her kind enthusiasm for this work and for generously sharing her immense knowledge.

My wife and children, all of whom patiently made sacrifices so that I could focus on this project.

Rev. Lance Quinn for his relentless encouragement for me to point God's people to truth.

Introduction

A biographical sketch of John Newton

Imagine the most hardened juvenile delinquent you have ever seen, multiply that image by ten, and you will have some idea of what John Newton was like before he became a Christian. Surely no one who knew Newton as a young lad would ever have dreamed that this teenage rebel, profane sailor, naval deserter and slave-trader would ever be converted to Christ — much less that he would one day write the lyrics to one of the best-known hymns of all time, 'Amazing Grace'. The incredible story of how such a notorious sinner became an equally noteworthy pastor and a leader of the Evangelical movement in eighteenth-century England is simply astounding.

While this book includes numerous incidents from Newton's life, as well as insights into the cultural, historical and theological contexts in which he ministered, it is not a biography. Rather, it is an anthology — a topical, rather than chronological, arrangement of some of Newton's gentle pastoral wisdom. This compilation is taken from Newton's letters, which offer profound, compassionate counsel; from his sermons, filled with passionate evangelistic pleas and fiery challenges for Christians; and from his hymns, which are characterized by incredible spiritual transparency. Since some familiarity with the basic framework of Newton's life will be helpful to the reader, I have included a brief biographical sketch below.

John Newton was born on 24 July 1725 to Captain John and Elizabeth Newton. Captain Newton was not a Christian and, as a merchant trader, was often away from his wife and young son for months at a time. Newton wrote of his emotionally distant relationship with his father, 'He always observed an air of distance and severity in his carriage, which overawed and discouraged my spirit. I was always in fear before him…'[1] Newton's mother, on the other hand, was a dedicated believer who faithfully taught her only child the Word of God. At her knee, Newton learned to read and memorized Scripture passages, catechisms, hymns and poems. It was her hope that her son might one day become a preacher of the gospel. When she died, shortly before Newton's seventh birthday, his happy childhood died with her, and so did any Christian influence on his young heart.

After a few unsuccessful years at boarding school, the young Newton began accompanying his father on sailing expeditions to the Mediterranean. On board, he slept and took all his meals with his father, but the majority of his waking hours were spent in the company of sinful sailors who did nothing but further erode the influence of his mother's spiritual input. Over the next few tumultuous years, Newton squandered his father's numerous attempts to provide him with settled career opportunities. Due to his own foolishness, he was forced into service in the navy and was severely whipped following an attempted desertion. Shortly afterwards he transferred to a civilian slave-trading ship. Some time later, while apprenticed to land-based slave-traders in Africa, he suffered such cruel mistreatment that even the slaves pitied him. During these troubled years, Newton continued to vacillate between rigorous attempts at religious self-reformation and ever-deepening descents into wickedness and disdain for the gospel. These undulations between such vastly differing spiritual extremes eventually gave way to a life of unbridled sin and a blasphemous rejection of Christ.

It was during a near shipwreck in the North Atlantic that the Lord began to awaken Newton's calloused conscience. Following his almost miraculous return to Ireland, he once again experienced a short-lived burst of religious zeal. Some months later, on an island off the west coast of Africa, he became so ill (probably from malaria) that he was fearful that he might not recover. Almost delirious with a violent fever, Newton crept to a quiet place on the island to pray.

Here, in seclusion, he offered God no new promises of self-improvement, as he had done so many times in the past. Instead, he cast himself before the Lord, to do with him as he would please and, by God's amazing grace, he was 'enabled to hope and to believe in a crucified Saviour'. This turning from reliance on his own strenuous religious efforts to trusting solely in the perfect work of Christ was the most crucial moment in Newton's life, for this, surely, was the moment of his conversion. Newton said that the result of this humble confession of his own inability to save himself and his simple faith in the adequacy of Christ to save lost sinners was that 'The burden was removed from my conscience, and not only my peace, but my health was restored.'

Not long after his conversion, Newton married Mary Catlett, whom he had loved since he was seventeen years old. The newly-weds spent many months apart from one another, as Newton was now master of his own slave-trading vessel. It would be years before his conscience would be awakened to the evil of the slave trade. At this point in history, the grizzly business was regarded as culturally acceptable.

An unprecedented seizure, the night before Newton was to depart on another slave-trading voyage, left him unfit for travel and his sailing days were brought to an abrupt end. He never had another seizure in his life. Following a period of unemployment, Newton became a customs official for the busy port of Liverpool, a post that he would hold for almost a decade. It was during these years that he began to have the desire to become a preacher of the gospel.

After initial disappointments, he was ordained by the Bishop of Lincoln and was appointed as the curate of Olney, a poor parish in rural Buckinghamshire. Many of the people in Olney were illiterate lacemakers who practised their intricate trade in lowly cottages. In order to pass the time while they worked, lacemakers often recited or chanted to one another rhyming stories, or poems, called 'tells'. It was hearing these 'tells' as he passed the windows of homes in and around Olney that gave Newton the idea of writing new, spiritual, 'tells' for the people of his church. If they could not read, they certainly possessed a great capacity for memorizing, and he was determined to give them something worth chanting. It was these poems that would eventually become Newton's great hymns and, together with William Cowper's contributions, would make up the now famous collection known as the *Olney Hymns*.

During the sixteen years of Newton's ministry in Olney, many came to know Christ. A gallery, or balcony, had to be added to the church in order to accommodate the many who desired to hear him preach. In addition to the *Olney Hymns*, during these years Newton also published his autobiographical account of his conversion, entitled *An Authentic Narrative*, as well as a group of his letters offering pastoral counsel under the pen-name 'Omicron'. John and Mary had no children of their own, but during their ministry in Olney they adopted Mary's orphaned niece, Betsy, who was deeply cherished by them both.

Newton eventually became the minister of a congregation in London, where he would labour for twenty-eight years. Again a gallery was built to allow the growing congregation, including many new converts, to hear him preach. In addition to preaching and publishing, Newton became a mentor to a number of young men in the ministry, often inviting them into his home to join with the family and servants for morning family worship, followed by an informal time of questions and answers.

Notable among those whom the Lord was pleased to draw to himself under Newton's ministry in London was William Wilberforce, the parliamentarian who was ultimately responsible for the abolition of slavery in England. In order to assist Wilberforce's efforts, Newton published his *Thoughts upon the African Slave Trade*, in which he states, 'If my testimony should not be necessary or serviceable, yet perhaps, I am bound to shame myself by a public confession, which however sincere, comes too late to prevent or repair the misery and mischief to which I have, formerly, been accessory.'

In his later years, Newton came to be looked up to as a patriarch and spokesman for evangelicalism. He continued to preach into his eighties, even after becoming blind. In his last days, when confined to bed, he spoke of his trust in God's purposes and his gratitude for the certainty of his salvation in Christ, and his words were filled with many allusions to Scripture. He died on 21 December 1807, with his dear adopted daughter Betsy and her husband at his side, and was buried beside his beloved wife Mary, who had preceded him in death some seventeen years earlier.

Newton was a devoted husband, an example to all fathers, a loyal friend and a dedicated pastor. While his legacy does not include any massive theological works, he did leave behind a simple, yet beautiful, record of one pastor's consistent and sincere ministry, in the form of heartfelt hymns which are brimming with humble praise to God, powerful sermons which were lovingly crafted with the needs of a specific congregation in mind, and tender letters full of profound pastoral counsel. The fruit of Newton's ministry is worthy of our consideration today. It was rightly said of him that 'It was his *goodness* rather than his *greatness* that rendered him so especially attractive — the abundance of the grace of God that was in him.'[2]

1.

SO GREAT SALVATION

Saved by blood, I live to tell
What the love of Christ hath done;
He redeemed my soul from hell,
Of a rebel made a son.

Glory and honor to the One in three ;
To God the Father, Son, and Holy Ghost,
As was, and is, and evermore shall be.

A Table to the Third Book.

According to the Order and Subject of the Hymns.

I. Solemn Addresses to sinners.

	Hymn
Expostulation	1
Alarm	2
We were once as you are	3
Prepare to meet God	4
Invitation	5

II. Seeking, Pleading and Hoping.

The burdened sinner	6
Behold I am vile	7
The shining light	8
Encouragement	9
The waiting soul	10
The effort	11, 12
Seeking the beloved	13
Rest for weary souls	14

III. CONFLICT.

Light shining out of darkness	15
Welcome cross	16
Afflictions sanctified by the word	17
Temptation	18
Looking upwards in a storm	19

III. CONFLICT.

	Hymn
Valley of the shadow of death	20
The storm hushed	21
Help in time of need	22
Peace after a storm	23
Mourning & longing	24
Rejoice the soul of thy Servant	25
Self-acquaintance	26
Bitter and sweet	27
Prayer for patience	28
Submission	29
Why should I complain ?	30
Return, O Lord, how long !	31
Cast down, but not destroyed	32
The benighted traveller	33
The prisoner	34
Perplexity relieved	35
Prayer answered by crosses	36
I will trust and not be afraid	37
Questions to unbelief	38
Great effects by small means	39

Facsimile of a page from the *Olney Hymns,* including the titles of
several hymns quoted in this book

Newton's own conversion

This rebel made a son

The terms 'rebel' and 'wretch' are used by Newton in several of his hymns to describe the darkness of his heart without Christ. The following excerpts from his autobiography easily demonstrate that such terms were by no means an exaggeration. His candour concerning his genuine love of sin and utter disdain for, and blasphemy against, God show why such descriptive labels were appropriate.

I think, I took up and laid aside a religious profession three or four different times before I was sixteen years of age; but all this while my heart was insincere. I often saw a necessity of religion as a means of escaping hell; but I loved sin, and was unwilling to forsake it...

I was so strangely blind and stupid that sometimes, when I had been determined upon things which I knew were sinful and contrary to my duty, I could not go on quietly till I had first dispatched my ordinary task of prayer, in which I have grudged every moment of my time; and when this was finished, my conscience was in some measure pacified, and I could rush into folly with little remorse...

My delight, and habitual practice, was wickedness...

I not only sinned with a high hand myself, but made it my study to tempt and seduce others upon every occasion: nay, I eagerly sought occasion sometimes to my own hazard and hurt...

I had a little of that unlucky wit which can do little more than multiply troubles and enemies to its possessor; and upon some imagined affront I made a song in which I ridiculed [the ship's captain], his ship, his designs, and his person, and soon taught it to the whole ship's company. Such was the ungrateful return I made for his offers of friendship and protection. I had mentioned no names, but the allusion was plain, and he was no stranger either to the intention or the author... I ... was the willing slave of every evil, possessed with a legion of unclean spirits...

My whole life, when awake, was a course of most horrid impiety and profaneness. I know not that I have ever since met so daring a blasphemer; not content with common oaths and imprecations, I daily invented new ones; so that I was often seriously reproved by the captain, who was himself a very passionate man and not at all circumspect in his expressions.

In a word, I seemed to have every mark of final impenitence and rejection; neither judgements nor mercies made the least impression on me.

(*An Authentic Narrative*, Letters 2, 3, 4, 7)

In the hymn which follows, Newton 'sings' his testimony. These lyrics model for each of us the humble gratitude, exuberant joy and tremendous confidence in the finished work of Christ that should characterize the worship of every child of God.

Hear what he has done for my soul!

S aved by blood, I live to tell
What the love of Christ hath done;
He redeemed my soul from hell,
Of a rebel made a son.
Oh, I tremble still to think
How secure I lived in sin,
Sporting on destruction's brink,
Yet preserved from falling in.

In his own appointed hour,
To my heart the Saviour spoke,
Touched me by his Spirit's power,
And my dangerous slumber broke.
Then I saw and owned my guilt;
Soon my gracious Lord replied:
'Fear not, I my blood have spilt;
'Twas for such as thee I died.'

Shame and wonder, joy and love
All at once possessed my heart;
Can I hope thy grace to prove,
After acting such a part?
'Thou hast greatly sinned,' he said,
'But I freely all forgive;
I myself the debt have paid;
Now I bid thee rise and live.'

Come, my fellow-sinners, try;
Jesus' heart is full of love;
Oh that you, as well as I,
May his wondrous mercy prove!
He has sent me to declare,
All is ready, all is free;

Why should any soul despair,
When he saved a wretch like me?

(*Olney Hymns*, Book 3, Hymn 54)

Suggested Scripture readings: Jeremiah 17:9-10; Romans
5:8-10; Ephesians 2:1-10; Colossians 1:21-23

---

*'Come and hear, all who fear God, and I will tell of what he has
done for my soul'* (Ps. 66:16).

Through many dangers

In Newton's famous hymn 'Amazing Grace', he described himself as having passed 'through many dangers, toils and snares'. The dangers to which he refers were not only spiritual difficulties, but physical ones as well. His pre-conversion life was, if nothing else, a sequence of one amazing near-death experience after another. The following are a few examples.

The Lord preserved Newton from drowning when, following a drinking contest on a ship, he nearly jumped overboard to recover his fallen hat. He was protected from a shooting accident in which a gunshot went off so near to his face that it burned away a part of his hat. One night, Newton was lost in a dense, swampy jungle just off the coast of Africa and he found his way back to his ship by moonlight. On another occasion he was kept from drowning when the ship's captain suddenly and inexplicably ordered him to get out of a small boat that was about to leave the ship, putting another man in his place. The boat sank that night and the man who had been sent in his place died. Newton survived the severe ill-treatment he received at the hands of his employer's African mistress, which included deprivation of food or proper clothing, and exposure to the elements for days at a time. He was in fact treated worse than the slaves around him. Later, when Newton himself was the captain of a slave-trading vessel, the Lord protected him from harm during planned mutinies from crew members and insurrections from slaves.

There is certainly no more dramatic example of God's preservation of Newton's life than the miraculous deliverance from a North Atlantic storm so violent that even experienced sailors gave up any hope of survival. However, the Lord spared Newton and used this terrifying tempest to awaken his conscience from slumber and begin the process of drawing this profane sailor to himself. Some contemporary biographers over-simplify the process of Newton's conversion and report, in contradiction to Newton's own words, that he was converted during this horrific storm. The truth is that, while the fear induced by the storm did make him more sober and motivated him to begin reading the Scriptures, his efforts at self-reform were short-lived. A few months after the storm, Newton's life would prove that he was still a slave to sin. Below is his own account of the storm that the Lord used to begin awakening his dead soul.

I went to bed that night in my usual security and indifference, but was awaked from a sound sleep by the force of a violent sea which broke on board us; so much of it came down below as filled the cabin I lay in with water. This alarm was followed by a cry from the deck, that the ship was going down or sinking ... [and] we soon found the ship was filling with water very fast. The sea had torn away the upper timbers on one side, and made the ship a mere wreck in a few minutes...

Taking in all circumstances, it was astonishing, and almost miraculous, that any of us survived to relate the story. We had immediate recourse to the pumps; but the water increased against our efforts... With a common cargo, she must have sunk of course; but we had a great quantity of beeswax and wood on board, which were specifically lighter than the water...

We expended most of our clothes and bedding to stop the leaks (though the weather was exceedingly cold, especially to us, who had so lately left a hot climate); over these we nailed pieces of boards, and at last perceived the water abate... Indeed, I expected that every time the vessel descended in the sea, she would rise no more; and though I dreaded death now, and my heart foreboded [i.e. feared] the worst, if the Scriptures, which I had long since opposed, were indeed true; yet still I was but half convinced, and remained for a space of time in a sullen frame, a mixture of despair and impatience. I thought, if the Christian religion were true, I could not be forgiven; and was, therefore, expecting, and almost at times wishing, to know the worst of it...

After nine hours at the pumps and a short rest, the narrative continues:

I went to the helm, and steered the ship till midnight, excepting a small interval for refreshment. I had here leisure and convenient opportunity for reflection. I began to think of my former religious professions; the extraordinary turns in my life; the calls, warnings, and deliverances I had met with; the licentious course of my conversation [i.e. lifestyle], particularly my unparalleled effrontery in making the gospel history (which I could not now be sure was false, though I was not yet assured it was true) the constant subject of profane ridicule. I thought, allowing the Scripture premises, there never was, nor could be, such a sinner as myself; and then, comparing the advantages I had broken through, I concluded, at first, that my sins were too great to be forgiven...

I began to pray; I could not utter the prayer of faith; I could not draw near to a reconciled God, and call him Father: my prayer was like the cry of the ravens, which yet the Lord does not disdain to hear. I now began to think of that Jesus whom I had so often derided: I recollected the particulars of his life and of his death — a death for sins not his own, but, as I remembered, for the sake of those

who, in their distress, should put their trust in him. And
now I chiefly wanted evidence...

The great question now was, how to obtain faith ... how
I should gain an assurance that the Scriptures were of divine inspiration, and a sufficient warrant for the exercise of
trust and hope in God. One of the first helps I received (in
consequence of a determination to examine the New Testament more carefully) was from Luke 11:13 ... here I found
a Spirit spoken of, which was to be communicated [i.e.
given] to those who ask it. Upon this I reasoned thus: 'If this
book is true, the promise in this passage must be true likewise; I have need of that very Spirit, by which the whole
was written, in order to understand it aright. He has engaged [i.e. promised] here to give that Spirit to those who
ask. I must therefore pray for it, and, if it is of God, he will
make good his own word.' My purposes were strengthened
further by John 7:17. I concluded from thence that, though I
could not say from my heart that I believed the gospel, yet I
would, for the present, take it for granted; and that, by
studying it in this light, I should be more and more confirmed in it...

The wind was now moderate, but continued fair, and we
were still drawing nearer to our port. We began to recover
from our consternation, though we were greatly alarmed by
our circumstances. We found that, the water having floated
all our movables in the hold, all the casks of provisions had
been beaten to pieces by the violent motion of the ship...
The sails, too, were mostly blown away, so that we advanced but slowly, even while the wind was fair. We imagined ourselves about a hundred leagues from the land, but
were in reality much further. Thus we proceeded with an
alternate prevalence of hope and fear. My leisure time was
chiefly employed in reading and meditation on the Scriptures, and praying to the Lord for mercy and instruction...

Many days later, Newton tells us:

> We saw the island Tory, and the next day anchored in
> … Ireland … four weeks after the damage was sustained
> by the sea. When we came into this port our very last vict-
> uals were boiling in the pot; and before we had been there
> two hours, the wind, which seemed to have been providen-
> tially restrained till we were in a place of safety, began to
> blow with great violence, so that if we had continued at sea
> that night in our shattered, enfeebled condition, we must,
> in all human appearance, have gone to the bottom.
>
> (*An Authentic Narrative*, Letters 7, 8)

S **uggested Scripture reading:** Psalm 107

'Those who go down to the sea in ships,
Who do business on great waters;
They have seen the works of the LORD,
And his wonders in the deep'

(Ps. 107:23-24).

No more resolves

The genuine conversion of Newton (as opposed to his several mere
professions of faith) took place when he finally ceased making
promises *to God* about how he would improve himself spiritually,
and began to trust in the promise made *by God* about how he could
become perfectly righteous through faith in the finished work of
Christ. What incredible divine irony that Newton's cry for salvation
took place off the coast of Africa, kneeling on the very shores of the

islands where he himself had been held captive and had been treated so horribly that he was even pitied by the slaves! Speaking of the work the Lord did in his heart as a result of the storm, Newton wrote:

> Thus far the Lord had wrought a marvellous thing: I was no longer an infidel [i.e. an irreligious person]; I heartily renounced my former profaneness; I had taken up some right notions, was seriously disposed, and sincerely touched with a sense of the undeserved mercy I had received, in being brought safe through so many dangers. I was sorry for my misspent life, and purposed an immediate reformation: I was quite freed from the habit of swearing, which seemed to have been deeply rooted in me, as a second nature. Thus to all appearance, I was a new man.
>
> But although I cannot doubt that this change, so far as it prevailed, was wrought by the Holy Spirit and the power of God, yet still I was greatly deficient in many respects. I was in some degree affected with a sense of my more enormous sins, but I was little aware of the innate evils of my heart... I acknowledged the Lord's mercy in pardoning what was past, but depended chiefly upon my own resolution to do better for the time to come. I had no Christian friend or faithful minister to advise me that my strength was no more than my righteousness... From this period I could no more mock at sin, or jest with holy things; I no more questioned the truth of Scripture, or lost a sense of the rebukes of my conscience. Therefore I consider this as the beginning of my return to God, or rather, of his return to me; but I cannot consider myself to have been a believer (in the fullest sense of the word) till a considerable time afterwards...
>
> I was now a serious professor [i.e. making a serious profession of being a Christian], went twice a day to the prayers at church, and determined to receive the sacrament the next opportunity... I arose very early, was very particular and earnest in my private devotion; and, with

the greatest solemnity, engaged myself to be the Lord's for ever, and only his. This was not a formal, but a sincere surrender, under a warm sense of mercies recently received... Though my views of the gospel salvation were very indistinct, I experienced a peace and satisfaction in the ordinance that day, to which I had been hitherto a perfect stranger...

I set some value upon the Word of God, and was no longer a libertine; but my soul still cleaved to the dust. Soon ... I began to ... grow slack in waiting upon the Lord; I grew vain and trifling in my conversation [i.e. lifestyle]; and though my heart smote me often, yet my armour was gone, and I declined fast ... I seemed to have forgotten all the Lord's mercies, and my own engagements [i.e. promises] and was (profaneness excepted) almost as bad as before. The enemy prepared a train of temptations, and I became his easy prey; and, for about a month, he lulled me asleep in a course of evil, of which, a few months before, I could not have supposed myself any longer capable...

Sin first deceives, and then it hardens. I was now fast bound in chains; I had little desire, and no power at all to recover myself. I could not but at times reflect how it was with me; but if I attempted to struggle with it, it was in vain...

At length the Lord, whose mercies are infinite ... interposed to save me. He visited me with a violent fever, which broke the fatal chain, and once more brought me to myself. But, oh, what a prospect! I thought myself now summoned away. My past dangers and deliverances, my earnest prayers in the time of trouble, my solemn vows before the Lord at his table, and my ungrateful returns for all his goodness were all present to my mind at once. Then I began to wish that the Lord had suffered [i.e. allowed] me to sink into the ocean, when I first besought his mercy. For a little while,

I concluded the door of hope to be quite shut; but this continued not long. Weak, and almost delirious, I arose from my bed, and crept to a retired [place]; and here I found a renewed liberty to pray. I durst [i.e. dared] make no more resolves, but cast myself before the Lord, to do with me as he should please. I do not remember that any particular text, or remarkable discovery, was presented to my mind; but in general I was enabled to hope and believe in a crucified Saviour. The burden was removed from my conscience, and not only my peace, but my health was restored... And from that time, I trust, I have been delivered from the power and dominion of sin, though, as to the effects and conflicts of sin dwelling in me, I still 'groan, being burdened'. I now began again to wait upon the Lord; and though I have often grieved his Spirit, and foolishly wandered from him since (When, alas! shall I be more wise?), yet his powerful grace has hitherto preserved me from such black declensions as this I have last recorded; and I humbly trust in his mercy and promises, that he will be my guide and guard to the end.

(*An Authentic Narrative*, Letters 9, 10)

Looking at the cross

*I*n evil long I took delight,
Unawed by shame or fear;
Till a new object struck my sight,
And stopped my wild career.

I saw one hanging on a tree,
In agonies and blood;
Who fixed his languid eyes on me,
As near his cross I stood.

Sure, never till my latest breath,
Can I forget that look;

It seemed to charge me with his death,
Though not a word he spoke.

My conscience felt, and owned the guilt,
And plunged me in despair;
I saw my sins his blood had spilt,
And helped to nail him there.

Alas! I knew not what I did,
But now my tears are vain;
Where shall my trembling soul be hid?
For I the Lord have slain.

A second look he gave, which said,
'I freely all forgive;
This blood is for thy ransom paid;
I die, that thou mayst live.'

Thus, while his death my sin displays,
In all its blackest hue,
(Such is the mystery of grace)
It seals my pardon too.

With pleasing grief and mournful joy,
My spirit now is filled;
That I should such a life destroy,
Yet live by him I killed.

(*Olney Hymns*, Book 2, Hymn 57)

As a pastor, over the years I have spoken with many believers who are more than a little self-conscious that their testimony involves a process rather than a single dramatic event. If that is the case with you, then take heart at the way Newton describes his own conversion. Defining the moment of one's salvation, for some (including myself), is like trying to define the exact moment of a sunrise. The coming of the dawn's first light is so gradual that all that one knows for sure is that, while everything used to be shrouded in darkness, now it is bathed in light!

S uggested Scripture reading: Philippians 3:4-12

'... *that I may gain Christ, and may be found in him, not having a righteousness of my own derived from the law, but that which is through faith in Christ'* (Phil. 3:8-9).

The love of God

His boundless patience

The sermon quoted below is one that Newton preached in London on 19 December 1797, on a national 'Day of Thanksgiving to Almighty God for our late Naval Victories'. He chose for his text Hosea 11:8-9, one of the most moving statements of God's unconditional love for his undeserving people in the whole of the Old Testament. These particular verses stand in stark contrast to the first ten chapters of Hosea, which contain vivid documentation of Israel's gross sin and prediction of God's fiery judgement. But chapter 11 is the pivotal point of the book. In it, God expresses his deep, tender love for his spiritually adulterous people and asks the remarkable questions: 'How can I give you up…? How can I surrender you …?' (v. 8). When I reached this passage in my study of Hosea, I remember saying to myself, 'Lord, how can you *not* give them up after all the ways that they have sinned against you? How can you *not* judge them severely?' God's answer is grounded ultimately in his own character:

> My heart is turned over within me,
> All my compassions are kindled…
> For I am God and not man, the Holy One in your midst
>
> (Hosea 11:8-9).

As you read Newton's thoughts on this wonderful portion of Scripture, consider your own spiritual unfaithfulness and rejoice in the unconditional love and boundless patience of God.

Two reasons are assigned ... why [God] should still exercise longsuffering towards those who so justly deserve to perish. First, 'I am God and not man'; the patience of man, or of any mere creature, would have been overcome long ago by the perverseness of Israel; but he who made them, and he only, was able to bear with them still...

The people of Israel were for a time in a state of hard bondage, and were severely oppressed in Egypt. The Lord brought them out from hence with a mighty hand and stretched-out arm. He afterwards drowned Pharaoh and his host in the Red Sea; but he led Israel safely through the deep as upon dry land. In the barren wilderness he fed them with manna, and brought them water out of the rock. In the pathless wilderness he guided them, by a cloud in the day, and by a fire in the night. He fought their battles, subdued their enemies, and put them in possession of the land he had promised to their forefathers. They were a people whom the Most High elected for himself, as his peculiar treasure...

What returns did Israel make to the Lord for all these benefits? The history of their conduct is little more than the recital of a long series of ungrateful murmurings, disobedience, and rebellion. They resisted his will, broke his commandments, mingled with the heathens, and learned their ways. They repeatedly forsook the Lord God of their fathers, worshipped dumb idols, and practised all the abominations of the nations which the Lord had cast out before them...

Can we wonder, if justice demanded the utter ... ruin of a people so highly favoured, so well instructed, so often chastised and delivered, yet so incorrigibly ungrateful, daring, and obstinate? Is it not rather wonderful to hear the Lord expressing a reluctance to execute the sentence so justly deserved, and saying of such a people, 'How shall I give thee up?'

But can we read the history of Israel, without remarking how strongly it resembles our own? Have we not been equally distinguished from the nations around us, by spiritual and temporal blessings and by gross misimprovement [i.e. misuse] of them? …

If we had offended men, or angels, as we have offended our Creator and Redeemer, and had they permission and power to punish us, our case would be utterly desperate. Only he who made us is able to bear with us. All the attributes (as we speak) of the infinite God must of course be equally infinite. As is his majesty, so is his mercy. What is the puny power of man, compared with that almighty power which formed and upholds the immense universe? The disproportion is greater than that between a single drop of water and the boundless ocean. Thus his thoughts are higher than ours, as the heavens are higher than the earth. Who can set bounds to the exercise of his patience?

Secondly, 'I am the Holy One in the midst of thee.' In that dark and degenerate day, when the bulk of the nation was in a state of revolt and rebellion, there were a hidden remnant who feared and worshipped the Lord, and who mourned for the abominations which they could not prevent. Of these the Lord was mindful, and for the sake of these, deserved judgements were suspended from falling upon the rest…

The ship in which Paul sailed to Italy was preserved from sinking, though apparently in the utmost danger, because the apostle was on board her. Not only was this servant of God as safe in a storm at sea as if he had been on shore, but, for his sake, the Lord preserved the lives of all who were in the vessel.

('Motives to Humiliation and Praise', a sermon preached in the parish church of St Mary Woolnoth)

S uggested Scripture readings: Hosea 11:1-11; Ezra 9:5-15

'I am God and not man, the Holy One in your midst' (Hosea 11:9).

Plenteous redemption

The sermon excerpts below are taken from a collection of six messages which Newton published following his first, unsuccessful attempt to become ordained as a minister in the Church of England. The stated reason for the refusal of his application for ordination was that he did not have a university education. However, the church laws did make allowance for exceptions, and Newton and others thought that the real reason for this decision was that he was suspected of Methodism and 'enthusiasm', presumably because of his relationship with Wesley and his free association with other Dissenting believers. When he made a second appeal to the Archbishop of York he was told, 'His Grace thinks it best for you to continue in that station which providence has placed you in.'[1] The rejection caused him real embarrassment in Liverpool, where he continued in his government post as a senior customs official. You can hear his disappointment in the preface when he states:

The following discourses were drawn up about twelve months since, when I expected a speedy opportunity of delivering them from the pulpit. As the views I then had are now overruled, I take this method of laying them before the public that those who have thought proper to foretell the part I would have acted, if my desires had taken place, may be satisfied or silenced.

Yet I should not have thought it worth my while to give either myself or others this trouble, merely for my own vindication. Attempts of this kind usually imply too much of a man's importance to himself, to be either acceptable or successful...

The true reasons therefore of this publication are: the importance of the subjects treated of; and the probability that upon this occasion, many persons who have not yet considered them with the attention they deserve may be induced (some from a motive of friendship, and others from curiosity) to read what might appear in my name...

But Newton did not give up: 'As to laying aside all thoughts of the ministry, it is quite out of my power; I cannot, I will not give up the desire; though I hope I shall not run before I am sent.'[2] With the help of the influential Lord Dartmouth, he was ordained several years later as the curate-in-charge in Olney.

Think not to satisfy the divine justice by any poor performances of your own; think not to cleanse or expiate the evil of your hearts by any of your own inventions; but, 'behold the Lamb of God, which taketh away the sin of the world' (John 1:29). He died, that you may live; he lives, that you may live for ever. Put, therefore, your trust in the Lord; for with him is plenteous redemption. His sufferings and death are a complete final propitiation for sin. 'He is able to save to the uttermost'; and he is as willing as he is able. It was *this* [that] brought him down from heaven; for *this* he emptied himself of all glory, and submitted to all indignity. His humiliation expiates our pride; his perfect love atones for our ingratitude; his exquisite tenderness pleads for our insensibility.

He came to restore us to the favour of God; to reconcile us to ourselves, and to each other; to give us peace and joy in this life, hope and triumph in death, and after death glory, honour, and immortality. For he came, not merely to repair, and to restore, but to exalt; not only 'that we might have life', the life we had forfeited, but 'that we might have it abundantly' [John 10:10]; that our happiness might be more exalted, our title more firm, and our possession more secure than the state of Adam in paradise could boast, or than his posterity could have attained unto, if he had continued unsinning...

From the words, 'He spared not his own Son,' we may observe, in one view, the wonderful goodness and inflexible severity of God. So great was his goodness that, when man was by sin rendered incapable of *any* happiness, and obnoxious [i.e. exposed] to *all* misery, incapable of restoring himself, or of receiving the last assistance from any power in heaven or in earth, God spared not his only begotten Son, but in his unexampled love to the world, gave him, who alone was able to repair the breach... [God gave] this unspeakable gift of the Son of his love.

(*Six Sermons as Intended for the Pulpit*, Sermons 1, 2, 4)

Encouragement

M y soul is beset
With grief and dismay,
I owe a vast debt
And nothing can pay:
I must go to prison,
Unless that dear Lord,
Who died and is risen,
His pity afford.

The death that he died,
The blood that he spilt,
To sinners applied,
Discharge from all guilt:
This great Intercessor
Can give, if he please,
The vilest transgressor
Immediate release.

When nailed to the tree,
He answered the prayer
Of one who, like me,
Was nigh to despair;
He did not upbraid him
With all he had done,
But instantly made him
A saint and a son.

The jailer, I read,
A pardon received;
And how was he freed?
He only believed;
His case mine resembled,
Like me he was foul,
Like me too he trembled,
But faith made him whole.

Though Saul in his youth,
To madness enraged,
Against the Lord's truth,
And people, engaged,
Yet Jesus, the Saviour,
Whom long he reviled,
Received him to favour
And made him a child.

A foe to all good,
In wickedness skilled,
Manasseh with blood
Jerusalem filled;
In evil long hardened,
The Lord he defied,
Yet he too was pardoned,
When mercy he cried.

Of sinners the chief,
And viler than all —
The jailer or thief,
Manasseh or Saul —
Since they were forgiven
Why should I despair,
While Christ is in heaven,
And still answers prayer?

(Olney Hymns, Book 3, Hymn 9)

The effort

*C*heer up, my soul, there is a mercy seat
Sprinkled with blood, where Jesus answers prayer;
There humbly cast thyself, beneath his feet,
For never needy sinner perished there.

Lord, I am come! Thy promise is my plea,
Without thy word I durst [i.e. dare] not venture nigh;
But thou hast called the burdened soul to thee;
A weary, burdened soul, O Lord, am I!

Bowed down beneath a heavy load of sin,
By Satan's fierce temptations sorely pressed,
Beset without, and full of fears within,
Trembling and faint, I come to thee for rest.

Be thou my refuge, Lord, my hiding-place,
I know no force can tear me from thy side;
Unmoved I then may all accusers face,
And answer every charge with, 'Jesus died.'

Yes, thou didst weep, and bleed, and groan, and die;
Well hast thou known what fierce temptations mean;
Such was thy love, and now, enthroned on high,
The same compassions in thy bosom reign.

Lord, give me faith! He hears — what grace is this!
Dry up thy tears, my soul, and cease to grieve:
He shows me what he did, and who he is;
I must, I will, I can, I do believe.

(Olney Hymns, Book 3, Hymn 11)

Suggested **Scripture readings:** Romans 5:1-11; 1 John 1:5 –
2:2

'As far as the east is from the west, so far has he removed our
transgressions from us' (Ps. 103:12).

Wakened by the force of love

Newton preached this sermon from 2 Corinthians 5 entitled 'The
Constraining Influence of the Love of Christ' in the presence of the
Lord Mayor, aldermen and sheriffs of London on 30 March 1800 as
a benefit for the Langbourn-Ward Charity School. Some time later,
the school requested that the sermon be printed and at that time
Newton inserted the following disclaimer:

The preacher cannot publish this sermon as an exact copy of what he delivered from the pulpit. Some interval passed before he was desired to print it. His recollection is much impaired by age [seventy-five years]; and he had no notes to assist it; but the plan is the same. He hopes and believes that none of the leading sentiments are omitted, and the additions, if any, are but few. As it is, he commends the perusal to the candour of the reader, and the blessing of Almighty God.

In the message, Newton expounds on the unfathomable love of Christ that was the controlling motive behind the apostle Paul's ministry. The other sermon, letters and hymns that follow reflect the same themes.

The love of Christ was the apostle's chief motive: it constrained him … bore him along like a torrent, in defiance of labour, hardship, and opposition. Many of us know the force of love in social life, and feel a readiness to do, bear, or forbear much for those whom we greatly love. But there is no love to be compared with the love of Christ…

We may be ashamed of the faintness of our conceptions of this love… When we attempt to conceive of this love, in its origin, progress, and effects, we are soon overwhelmed, our thoughts are swallowed up, and we can only wonder and adore in silence. This love of Christ to sinners is inexpressible, unsearchable, and passing knowledge; it is an ocean without either bottom or shore.

(Sermon entitled 'The Constraining Influence of the
Love of Christ')

[God] so loved sinners, enemies, rebels, that, for their sakes, he abandoned and delivered up his beloved Son into the hands of wicked men, permitted him to be assaulted by the powers of darkness; yea, it pleased the Father himself to bruise him, and to make his soul an offering for sin. This is love without parallel, and beyond conception. We can only admire and say, 'Behold, what manner of love the Father hath bestowed on us' [1 John 3:1]. When Jesus Christ as crucified is clearly apprehended by faith, then we have the most convincing, the most affecting proof, that God is love.

(*Twenty Sermons Preached at Olney*, Sermon 8)

I dare not tell you, madam, what I am; but I can tell you what I wish to be. The love of God, as manifested in Jesus Christ, is what I would wish to be the abiding object of my contemplation; not merely to speculate upon it as a doctrine, but so to feel it, and my own interest in it, as to have my heart filled with its effects, and transformed into its resemblance.

(*Cardiphonia*, 'Seven Letters to Mrs ...', Letter 3)

The manifestation of the love of God to sinners is in Christ Jesus... And, oh, what love was this to give his own only Son! ... 'His own love': love peculiar to himself, and of which we can find no shadow or resemblance among creatures.

(*Letters intended as a sequel to Cardiphonia*, 'Fourteen Letters to the Rev. Dr ...,' Letter 8)

It is good to be here

Let me dwell on Golgotha,
Weep and love my life away!
While I see him on the tree
Weep and bleed, and die for me!

That dear blood, for sinners spilt,
Shows my sin in all its guilt:
Ah, my soul, he bore thy load,
Thou hast slain the Lamb of God.

Hark! His dying words: 'Forgive,
Father, let the sinner live;
Sinner, wipe thy tears away,
I thy ransom freely pay.'

While I hear this grace revealed,
And obtain a pardon sealed,
All my soft affections move,
Wakened by the force of love.

Farewell, world, thy gold is dross,
Now I see the bleeding cross;
Jesus died to set me free
From the law, and sin, and thee!

He has dearly bought my soul;
Lord, accept, and claim the whole!
To thy will I will resign,
Now no more my own, but thine.

(*Olney Hymns*, Book 2, Hymn 56)

Christ crucified

When, on the cross, my Lord I see,
Bleeding to death, for wretched me,
Satan and sin no more can move,
For I am all transformed to love.

His thorns, and nails, pierce through my heart,
In every groan I bear a part;
I view his wounds with streaming eyes;
But see! He bows his head and dies!

Come, sinners, view the Lamb of God,
Wounded and dead, and bathed in blood!

Behold his side, and venture near;
The well of endless life is here.

Here I forget my cares and pains;
I drink, yet still my thirst remains;
Only the fountain-head above
Can satisfy the thirst of love.

Oh, that I thus could always feel!
Lord, more and more thy love reveal!
Then my glad tongue shall loud proclaim
The grace and glory of thy name.

Thy name dispels my guilt and fear,
Revives my heart, and charms my ear,
Affords a balm for every wound,
And Satan trembles at the sound.

(Olney Hymns, Book 2, Hymn 54)

Suggested Scripture readings: Philippians 2:5-11;
2 Corinthians 5:14-15

'For the love of Christ controls us ... so that they who live might no longer live for themselves, but for him who died and rose again on their behalf' (2 Cor. 5:14-15).

Sovereign grace

A heart of stone

Throughout his ministry, Newton was unashamedly committed to the God-glorifying doctrines of grace. To him they were more than a creed; they were an integral part of his walk in relationship with God. He states in the preface to the *Olney Hymns*:

> The views I have received of the doctrines of grace are essential to my peace. I could not live comfortably a day or an hour without them. I likewise believe, yea, so far as my poor attainments warrant me to speak, I know them to be friendly to holiness, and to have a direct influence in producing and maintaining a gospel conversation [i.e. a lifestyle that befits the gospel], and therefore I must not be ashamed of them.

In contrast to many Calvinists, Newton fellowshipped freely with many who did not agree with all of his own doctrinal views. His friendship with John and Charles Wesley is perhaps the most notable example. Newton's generosity and humility regarding doctrine is captured in these two quotations:

> Though a man does not accord with my view of election, yet if he gives me good evidence that he is effectually called

of God, he is my brother… If he loves Jesus, I will love him, whatever hard name he may be called by, and whatever incidental mistakes I may think he holds. His differing from me will not always prove him wrong, except [i.e. since] I am fallible myself.

> *(Letters intended as a Sequel to Cardiphonia*, 'Eighteen Letters to the Rev. Mr S…,' Letter 18)

I hope I am upon the whole a *scriptural* preacher; for I find I am considered as an Arminian among the high Calvinists, and as a Calvinist among the strenuous Arminians.

> (Quoted by Cecil, *John Newton*, p.193)

Newton's love for the truth of God's sovereignty produced a loving humility not always characteristic of Calvinists in his day, or our own:

If you mean by a rigid Calvinist, one who is fierce, dogmatical, and censorious, and ready to deal out anathemas against all who differ from him, I hope I am no more such a one than I am a rigid papist. But, as to the doctrines which are now stigmatized by the name Calvinism, I cannot well avoid the epithet rigid, while I believe them: for there seems to be no medium between holding them and not holding them; between ascribing salvation to the will of man, or the power of God; between grace and works (Romans 11:6); between being found in the righteousness of Christ, or in my own (Philippians 3:9). Did the harsh consequences often charged upon the doctrine called Calvinism really belong to it, I should have much to answer for if I had invented it myself, or taken it upon trust from Calvin; but, as I find it in the Scriptures, I cheerfully embraced it, and leave it to the Lord to vindicate his own truths and his own ways, from all the imputations which have been cast upon them all.

> *(Letters intended as a Sequel to Cardiphonia*, 'Fourteen Letters to the Rev. Dr …,' Letter 13)

Regarding the way that he allowed the sweet truths of God's sovereignty in salvation to permeate all his ministry, Newton said in a conversation with William Jay, a fellow minister, ' "I am more a Calvinist than anything else; but I use my Calvinism in my writings and my preaching as I use this sugar." Newton then took a lump, and putting it into his teacup, and stirring it added, "I do not give it alone, and whole; but mixed and diluted." ' [3]

And permeate it did. The doctrines of grace also found their way into Newton's hymns. The one quoted below is based on the account in the Gospel of Luke of the two thieves who were crucified on either side of Jesus, and it powerfully illustrates what Newton sometimes liked to call the 'invincible grace' of God. In it, he addresses the difficult question of explaining how we account for the fact that, while one thief cried out for salvation and received merciful pardon, the other man scoffed at Jesus and died in his sins. Newton's poignant answer is: 'Sovereign grace'.

The two malefactors

Sovereign grace has power alone
To subdue a heart of stone;
And the moment grace is felt,
Then the hardest heart will melt.

When the Lord was crucified,
Two transgressors with him died;
One, with vile blaspheming tongue,
Scoffed at Jesus as he hung.

Thus he spent his wicked breath,
In the very jaws of death,
Perished, as too many do,
With the Saviour in his view.

But the other, touched with grace,
Saw the danger of his case;
Faith received to own the Lord,
Whom the scribes and priests abhorred.

'Lord,' he prayed, 'remember me,
When in glory thou shalt be.'
'Soon with me,' the Lord replies,
'Thou shalt rest in paradise.'

This was wondrous grace indeed,
Grace vouchsafed in time of need!
Sinners, trust in Jesu's name,
You shall find him still the same.

But beware of unbelief;
Think upon the hardened thief;
If the gospel you disdain,
Christ, to you, will die in vain.

(*Olney Hymns*, Book 1, Hymn 110)

Until I read this hymn, I had never considered how the close physical proximity of these men to Jesus Christ makes the reaction of the unrepentant thief all the more shocking. How sad to consider that this convicted criminal who, as he was dying, was close enough to Jesus to carry on a personal conversation with him actually perished without calling out to him for salvation!

This hymn is an encouraging reminder to persevere in praying for loved ones and friends who are not Christians. The thief who went to paradise with Christ is a wonderful example of the truth that, as one of my pastoral colleagues used to say to me, 'As long as there's breath, there's hope.' The thief, undergoing capital punishment for his crimes, hardly seemed a candidate for conversion. Yet God reached down in the last possible moment and wonderfully saved that man. I'm sure that there is someone on your prayer list who seems too hard-hearted ever to be saved. Don't stop praying! The thief on the cross is a reminder that it is never too late and that no heart is too hard to resist the sovereign grace of God.

Finally, this hymn serves as a warning regarding the sin of unbelief. Remember the thief who saw Christ with his own eyes and yet did not place his faith in the crucified Saviour. He heard the words, 'Father, forgive them ...', with his own ears, but did not seek forgiveness for his sins. Perhaps you are reading this book and you think that merely hearing the words of Christ by attending church or growing up in a Christian home will save you. Guard your heart from unbelief. Nearness to the things of Christ will not save you. Imitate the repentant thief who feared God, confessed his own sinfulness and placed his faith in Christ, the sinless Saviour, as his only hope.

Suggested **Scripture readings:** Luke 23:39-43; Romans 9:1-23

> *'And he said to him, "Truly I say to you, today you shall be with me in paradise"'* (Luke 23:43).

Grace reigns

I was shocked to overhear someone once say, 'I'm a Calvinist and proud of it!' I remember wondering how it was possible that the teaching which, more than any other in the entire Bible, deals a crushing blow to pride could produce such a statement. Learning of man's utter spiritual destitution and inability, and God's undeserved free mercy and grace, should induce worship, not arrogance. Such truths should cause us to rejoice in declaring that salvation, from beginning to end, belongs not to man, but to our God!

In this sermon based on Matthew 11:25-26, Newton explores the reasons why God the Father was pleased to hide spiritual truth from the 'wise' of this world and in turn reveal it to mere 'babes':

Besides the argument of his sovereignty, 'that so it has pleased him', he has been pleased to favour us with some of the reasons, 'why it has so pleased him'. And this is the subject I propose to lead our meditations to from these words...

1. The Lord of hosts hath proposed it, 'to stain the pride of all human glory' (Isaiah 23:9). How much men are disposed to admire their own wisdom, learning, and fancied accomplishments is sufficiently obvious. But now the pride of all this glory is stained, inasmuch as it is proved by experience to be utterly useless in the most important concerns... They are without Christ, and without hope: those things which alone are of real importance are [hidden] from their eyes. Here the desperate depravity and deceitfulness of the heart are manifested to the glory of God; and it is clearly seen that if he does not interpose to save, men are wholly unable to save themselves...

2. To exclude boasting... [If] men were saved, either in whole or in part, by their own wisdom and prudence, they might, in the same degree, ascribe the glory and praise to themselves. They might say, 'My own power and wisdom gave me this'; and thus God would be robbed of the honour due [to] his name...

3. This method of divine procedure opens a door of hope to the vilest and the meanest [i.e. lowest]. Let not any be cast down on account of any peculiar incapacity or difficulty in their case. If none but the wise and learned, the rich, and those who are esteemed well-behaved and virtuous could be saved, or if these stood in a fairer way for it than others, the greatest part of mankind might give up hope, and sit down in despair at once... You who are sensible [i.e. conscious that] you have nothing of your own to trust to, take encouragement; the Lord has suited his gospel to your circumstances...

4. In this way the salvation of believers is sure. If it depended on anything in man, it might miscarry... If this concern had been left to the wisdom of man, it is most probable that Christ would have lived and died in vain, without a single real disciple. But now the dispensation [i.e. dispensing] of grace is in his hands, we are sure that some

will believe in him; and we are likewise sure that those who truly do so shall never be ashamed of their hope.

Now, from what has been said, enquire what is the temper of your minds with regard to this appointment. Our Lord rejoiced in it as the wise and holy will, the good pleasure, of his heavenly Father. If you are displeased at it, is it not proof that you have not the mind which was in Christ Jesus? If God *wills* one thing, and you *will* another, where must the contention end? To what purpose, or with what pretence, can you use that expression in the Lord's Prayer, 'Thy will be done', when in effect your heart rises with enmity against it? … He is God, and who can control him? Who can say unto him, 'What hast thou done?' You must either submit to his golden sceptre in time, or his rod of iron will fall upon you for ever…

If you are most unworthy of mercy, and destitute of every plea, should you not be glad to hear that the Lord does not expect worthiness in those whom he saves, but that he himself has provided the only plea which he will accept, and a plea which cannot be overruled, the righteousness and mediation of his well-beloved Son?

(*Twenty Sermons Preached at Olney*, Sermon 5)

Reigning grace

*N*ow may the Lord reveal his face,
And teach our stammering tongues
To make his sovereign, reigning grace,
The subject of our songs!
No sweeter subject can invite
A sinner's heart to sing;
Or more display the glorious right
Of our exalted King.

This subject fills the starry plains
With wonder, joy, and love;
And furnishes the noblest strains
For all the harps above;
While the redeemed in praise combine
To grace upon the throne;
Angels in solemn chorus join,
And make the theme their own.

Grace reigns, to pardon crimson sins,
To melt the hardest hearts;
And from the work it once begins,
It never more departs.
The world and Satan strive in vain,
Against the chosen few;
Secured by grace's conquering reign,
They all shall conquer too.

Grace tills the soil, and sows the seeds,
Provides the sun and rain;
Till from the tender blade proceeds
The ripened harvest grain.
'Twas grace that called our souls at first,
By grace thus far we're come,
And grace will help us through the worst,
And lead us safely home.

Lord, when this changing life is past
If we may see thy face,
How shall we praise, and love, at last,
And sing the reign of grace!
Yet let us aim while here below
Thy mercy to display;

And own at least the debt we owe,
Although we cannot pay.

(*Olney Hymns*, Book 3, Hymn 86)

Suggested **Scripture readings:** Matthew 11:25-30; Romans 4:1-8; Revelation 19:1-4

'Yes, Father, for this way was well-pleasing in your sight'
(Matt. 11:26).

But now I see

The famous line from the hymn 'Amazing Grace', '... was blind, but now I see', is the gospel in a nutshell. Blindness is a perfect metaphor to describe the inability of our darkened hearts to perceive anything about our own spiritual danger without Christ. Sight is an equally powerful image for the believer's capacity to perceive the world around him after regeneration. The letter and sermon quoted below elaborate on the theme of God miraculously giving us eyes to see.

The reason why men in a natural state are utterly ignorant of spiritual truths is that they are wholly destitute of a faculty suited to perception... Those passages of Scripture wherein the gospel truth is compared to light lead to a familiar illustration of my meaning. Men by nature are stark blind with respect to this light; by grace the eyes of the understanding are opened... Nor can all the learning or study in the world enable any person to form a suitable judgement of divine truth, till the eyes of his mind are opened, and then he will perceive it at once...

Regeneration, or that great change without which a man cannot see the kingdom of God, is the effect of almighty power. Neither education, endeavours, nor arguments can open the eyes of the blind. It is God alone, who at first caused light to shine out of darkness, who can shine into our hearts, 'to give us the light of the knowledge of the glory of God in the face of Jesus Christ'. People may attain some natural ideas of spiritual truths by reading books, or hearing sermons, and may thereby become wise in their own conceits; they may learn to imitate the language of an experienced Christian; but they know not what they say, nor whereof they affirm, and are as distant from the true meaning of the terms as a blind man who pronounces the words 'blue' or 'red' is from the ideas which those words raise in the mind of a person who can distinguish colours by his sight.

And from hence we may infer the sovereignty, as well as the efficacy of grace; since it is evident, not only that the objective light, the Word of God, is not afforded universally to all men; but that those who enjoy the same outward means have not all the same perceptions. There are many who stumble in the noonday, not for want of light, but for the want of eyes; and they who now see were once blind even as others, and had neither power nor will to enlighten their own minds. It is a mercy, however, when people are so far sensible of their own blindness as to be willing to wait for the manifestation of the Lord's power, in the ordinances of his own appointment. He came into the world, and he sends forth his gospel, that those who see not may see; and when there is a desire in the heart for spiritual sight, it shall in his due time be answered...

[Where] the eyes are divinely enlightened, the soul's first view of itself and of the gospel may be confused and indistinct, like him who saw men as it were trees walking; yet this light is like the dawn, which, though weak and faint at its first appearance, shineth more and more unto the perfect day...

[Believers] have obtained a glimpse of the Redeemer's glory, as he is made unto us, of God, wisdom, righteousness, sanctification, and redemption, so that his name is precious, and the desire of their hearts is towards him...

A believer may be much in the dark; but his spiritual sight remains. Though the exercise of grace may be low, he knows himself, he knows the Lord, he knows the way of access to a throne of grace. His frames [i.e. mental states] and feelings may alter; but he has received such a knowledge of the person and offices, the power and grace, of Jesus the Saviour as cannot be taken from him; and he could withstand even an angel that should preach another gospel, because he has *seen* the Lord.

(*Forty-One Letters on Religious Subjects*, Letter 21)

They were once blind, but now they *see*. The religion of true believers is not the effect of imagination and blind impulse, but is derived from ... an enlightened understanding. They see God; their apprehensions of him are, in some measure, answerable to his greatness and his goodness, and inspire them with reverence and love... Sin appears to them hateful in itself, as well as mischievous in its consequences; and holiness, not only necessary by the ordination of God, but desirable for its own sake, as essentially belonging to the true dignity and happiness of man. They know themselves; they see and feel that they are such creatures as the Bible describes them to be — weak, depraved and vile. Of course they see the folly of attempting to recommend themselves to God, and can no longer place any dependence on what they once accounted their wisdom, power, or righteousness; and therefore they see the absolute necessity of a Saviour. They see, likewise, and approve the method of salvation proposed by the gospel, as worthy of the wisdom and justice of God, and every way adapted to the exigencies of their sins, wants, and fears. They see and admire the excellence, dignity, and sufficiency of him on whom their help is laid. His power and authority engage their confidence; his love captivates and fixes their hearts. They see the vanity of the present state, and the vast importance of eternity. In these respects they have all of them a good understanding, however inferior [they may be] in natural capacity, or acquired knowledge, to the wise men of the world.

(*Fifty Sermons on Handel's 'The Messiah'*, Sermon 12)

Suggested **Scripture** **readings:** John 12:37-50; 2 Corinthians 4:1-7

> *'The god of this world has blinded the eyes of the unbelieving so that they might not see the light of the gospel of the glory of Christ'*
> (2 Cor. 4:4).

Essentials in Christianity

Even with Newton's strong doctrinal convictions, he managed to be truly ecumenical in the best sense of the word. His ability to delineate clearly between primary and secondary doctrinal issues made it possible for him to enjoy the friendship of believers from various religious persuasions. He was himself a Calvinist, yet fellowshipped with the Methodists of his time. He was an Anglican, yet sometimes cancelled his own evening services in Olney and took his entire congregation to worship with the Baptists. He did not agree with all of Whitefield's teachings, yet deeply admired his preaching. Newton pursued a kind of warm-hearted unity that avoided two extremes: first, the kind of unity that is based on uniformity of doctrinal agreement, even in theological non-essentials; and, secondly, the sort of unity that ignores all doctrinal distinctions and that compromises on theological points that are crucial to the definition of Christianity. In the 'unity-at-any-price' age in which we live, we would do well to cling tenaciously to the essentials that Newton addresses below.

Essentials in Christianity are those things without which no man can be a Christian in the sight of God, and by the decision of his Word; and, on the other hand, those things only are essential which whoever possesses is, by Scripture declaration, in a state of favour with God through Christ. These might be branched out into many particulars; but they are fully and surely comprised in two – faith and holiness…

If the question is removed another step, and it should be asked, 'Which, or how many, of the doctrines of Scripture are necessary to produce the faith and holiness supposed [to be] requisite?' it may suffice to say, that, in the nature of things, no person can be expected to believe in Christ till convinced of his need of him, and of his ability, as a Saviour, fully to answer his expectations. And as a supreme love to God and a hatred of all sin are evidently included in the idea of holiness, it supposes [i.e. necessarily requires] a disposition of mind which every man's experience proves to be beyond the power of a fallen nature; and therefore a competent knowledge and cordial acceptance of what the Scripture teaches concerning the nature and desert [i.e. the just deserts] of sin, the person and mediatory acts of Christ, the causes, ends, and effects of his mediation, together with the necessity of that change of heart which is expressed by being born again, appear to be essentially necessary to that faith and holiness which are described in the gospel.

(*A Review of Ecclesiastical History*, chapter 2)

Indeed, the great points of immediate [concern] may be summed up in a few words: to have a real conviction of our sin and unworthiness; to know that Jesus is the all-sufficient Saviour, and that there is no other; to set him before us as our Shepherd, Advocate, and Master; to place our hope upon him alone; to live to him who lived and died for us; to wait in his appointed means for the consolations of his Spirit; to walk in his steps, and copy his character; and to be daily longing for the period [i.e. end] of our warfare, that we may see him as he is. All may be reduced to these heads [i.e. headings]; or the whole is better expressed in the apostle's summaries [in] Titus 2:11-14 and 3:3-8. But, though the lessons are brief, it is a great thing to attain any good measure of proficiency in them; yea, the more we advance, the more we shall be sensible [i.e. conscious of] how far we fall short of their full import.

(*Letters intended as a sequel to Cardiphonia*, 'Fourteen Letters to the Rev. Dr ...,' Letter 3)

I should think it no hard matter to draw up a form of sound words ... to which true believers of all sorts and sizes would unanimously subscribe. Suppose it ran something in the following manner:

I believe that sin is the most hateful thing in the world: that I and all men are by nature in a state of wrath and depravity, utterly unable to sustain the penalty or to fulfil the commands of God's holy law; and that we have no sufficiency of ourselves to think a good thought.

I believe that Jesus is the chief among ten thousands; that he came into the world to save the chief of sinners, by making Christ a propitiation for sin by his death, by paying a perfect obedience to the law on our behalf; and that he is now exalted on high, to give repentance and remission of sins to all that believe; and that he ever liveth to make intercession for us.

I believe that the Holy Spirit (the gift of God through Jesus Christ) is the sure and only guide into all truth, and the common privilege of all believers; and under his influence, I believe the Holy Scriptures are able to make us wise unto salvation, and to furnish us thoroughly for every good work.

I believe that love to God, and to man for God's sake, is the essence of religion, and the fulfilling of the law; that without holiness no man shall see the Lord; that those who, by a patient course in well-doing, seek glory, honour, and immortality shall receive eternal life: and I believe that this reward is not of debt, but of grace, even to the praise and glory of that grace whereby he has made us accepted in the Beloved. Amen.

(Cardiphonia, 'A Letter to the Rev. Mr O...')

Suggested **Scripture readings**: Ephesians 4:1-6; Titus 2:11 – 3:7

'... *being diligent to preserve the unity of the Spirit in the bond of peace*' (Eph. 4:3).

Assurance of salvation

Do I love the Lord?

In the first few years after his conversion, Newton had great struggles with assurance of his salvation. At times, he became lost in a labyrinth of introspection that led him to despair. He documents his spiritual unrest in his diary: 'Must this be the result of my enquiry into the state of my soul — to find myself going backwards instead of forwards?' He cried out to the Lord for 'a comfortable evidence within myself that I am thy real disciple'. [4]

The Lord principally used two men to relieve his spiritual dilemma. One was an evangelical sea captain, Alexander Clunie, who spent much time personally teaching Newton and praying with him. The other was David Jennings, the Dissenting pastor of the church that Newton's mother had attended, a man whom he grew to respect as a spiritual father. Under the influence of these two godly men, he found the peace which had eluded him so long. From these men he learned that assurance of salvation is enjoyed by those who not only examine their own hearts for *subjective* evidences of conversion, but also place their simple trust in the *objective*, unconditional, unchanging work of Christ on behalf of sinners. The importance of this balance is seen in virtually all of Newton's writings on this crucial topic.

Below is a striking hymn about Newton's personal battle with doubt, in which he confesses that he often had 'anxious thoughts' about his spiritual state and refers to himself as a 'doubtful case'. As with many of the *Olney Hymns*, a Bible reference is given below the title of the song, indicating the passage of Scripture that provided the stimulus for writing it. Often this was the text from which Newton was about to preach. In this case, it is taken from John 21:16. It is easy to imagine Newton in his attic study, looking out of the window to the spire of his church, meditating over this passage, in which Jesus asks Peter, 'Do you love me?' Perhaps, with quill in hand, Newton paused to ask himself the same penetrating question: 'Do I really love the Lord?' He permanently captured his answer to the question in the form of a hymn.

Lovest thou me?
John 21:16

'*T*is a point I long to know,
  Oft it causes anxious thought;
Do I love the Lord, or no?
Am I his, or am I not?

If I love, why am I thus?
Why this dull and lifeless frame?
Hardly, sure, can they be worse
Who have never heard his name!

Could my heart so hard remain,
Prayer a task and burden prove,
Every trifle give me pain,
If I knew a Saviour's love?

When I turn my eyes within,
All is dark, and vain, and wild;
Filled with unbelief and sin,
Can I deem myself a child?

If I pray, or hear, or read,
Sin is mixed with all I do;
You that love the Lord indeed,
Tell me, is it thus with you?

Yet I mourn my stubborn will,
Find my sin a grief and thrall [i.e. bondage];
Should I grieve for what I feel,
If I did not love at all?

Could I joy his saints to meet,
Choose the ways I once abhorred,
Find, at times, the promise sweet,
If I did not love the Lord?

Lord, decide the doubtful case!
Thou who art thy people's sun,
Shine upon thy work of grace,
If it be indeed begun.

Let me love thee more and more,
If I love at all, I pray;
If I have not loved before,
Help me to begin today.

(*Olney Hymns*, Book 1, Hymn 119)

The hymn is a model of the kind of spiritual candour that is so endearing in a spiritual leader. Can you imagine the courage required for a preacher to confess to his congregation that he himself at times had doubts of this kind? Such bold honesty must have provided encouragement, comfort and hope to his congregation. I know it has for me! No wonder the people of Olney loved their minister! Newton's courageous transparency remains, for me, one of the most remarkable and attractive characteristics of his writings.

Suggested Scripture readings: John 21:15-25; 1 John 2:3-11; 3:6-18; 5:1-5

> 'He said to him again a second time, "Simon, son of John, do you love me?" He said to him, "Yes, Lord; you know that I love you"'
> (John 21:16).

A solid, permanent assurance

In the autumn of 1767, a thirty-six-year-old bachelor named William Cowper moved to Olney. Cowper was a bashful, fragile, barrister-turned-poet from an aristocratic family who had struggled since childhood with frequent, serious bouts of depression. He had become a Christian while in an asylum under the gentle care of a godly physician, Dr Cotton. The sole purpose of Cowper's move to Olney, along with the family with whom he lodged, was to sit under the ministry of John Newton. In time Newton and Cowper became incredibly close friends. Cowper's residence, Orchard Side, and the vicarage where the Newtons lived were adjacent to one another, separated only by a small orchard. The proximity of their homes seemed a metaphor for the nearness of their hearts. Newton recalled that 'For nearly twelve years we were seldom separated for seven hours at a time when we were awake, and at home.'[5]

William Cowper

Cowper became an active member of the Newtons' church, regularly attending, and sometimes leading, weekly prayer meetings, visiting the sick, showing great concern for the poor lacemakers who were his neighbours. His zeal for good works, coupled with his knowledge of Scripture, made him a sort of informal curate to Newton. The patience and devotion shown by both John and Mary Newton towards this troubled young man is perhaps best exemplified by the hospitality shown to Cowper on the occasion when he found the noise from the annual town fair so disturbing that he went to spend the night at the vicarage with the Newtons, and ended up staying for fourteen months before he was able to go home!

As an aid to combating Cowper's depression, Newton encouraged him to use his literary gifts and join him in writing hymns for the Tuesday evening prayer meetings. Later those hymns would form part of the enduring collection known as the *Olney Hymns*. Newton states in his preface to the hymnal that one of the motives for the project was as 'a monument to perpetuate the remembrance of an intimate and enduring friendship' and expresses his sadness that there were not more hymns written by Cowper: 'We had not proceeded far upon our proposed plan, before my dear friend was prevented, by a long and affecting indisposition, from affording me further assistance. My grief and disappointment were great; I hung my harp upon the willows, and for some time thought myself determined to proceed no farther without him.'

Cowper's periods of depression were minimal for the first six years after moving to Olney, which he considered to be the most peaceful period in his life. But a crisis more severe than any he had yet experienced was looming. On New Year's Day 1773, Newton preached from I Chronicles 17:16-17 (presumably the sermon for which 'Amazing Grace' was written). Little did he suspect that this would be the last sermon that Cowper would ever hear. Cowper had tea in the vicarage with the Newtons that afternoon and later that evening wrote his most famous hymn, 'God Moves in a Mysterious Way'. The next morning, Newton was summoned to Cowper's home and found his friend inconsolably depressed and inexplicably suicidal.

A month after this crisis, Cowper had a terrifying nightmare, in which he was convinced that he heard the Lord tell him that there was no hope for him. This disturbing dream shook his confidence in the work of Christ on his own behalf. Somehow this man who wrote such beautiful hymns about the grace of God reached the conclusion that the gospel was true for others, but not for himself.

Cowper never fully recovered and continued to suffer for the remainder of his life. He was unwilling to go to the vicarage or attend public worship services. But Newton was faithful in often visiting him at Orchard Side and wrote that Cowper 'used to point with his finger to the church' and say, 'You know the comfort I have had there and how I have seen the glory of the Lord in his house and until I can go there I'll not go anywhere else.'[6]

Six years after that crisis, when Newton was called to move to London, he remained loyal to his friend. He asked William Bull, a friend and fellow minister from a nearby village, to take over the pastoral care of Cowper. The two men became friends and dined together at least once every two weeks. From a distance, Newton and Cowper continued their relationship by letter over the next twenty-seven years.

When Cowper died, in the spring of 1800, Newton preached his funeral sermon, choosing for his text the account of the Lord's appearing to Moses in the

William Bull

burning bush. He stated, 'I know no text in the whole of God's Word more suited to the case of my dear friend than that I have read. He was indeed a bush in flames for twenty-seven years but he was not consumed. And why? Because the Lord was there.'[7] Newton composed a few verses when he heard of Cowper's death; the last stanza reads:

Oh! Let thy memory awake!
I told thee thus would end thy heaviest woe,
I told thee that thy God would bring thee here,
And God's own hand would wipe away thy tear,
While I should claim a mansion by thy side;
I told thee so – for our Emmanuel died.
(Quoted in Edwards, *Through Many Dangers*, p. 260)

In addition to Newton's own experiences of spiritual doubt from his days as a new believer, no doubt his observance of Cowper's intense struggle influenced his preaching in Olney on the subject. The sermon and hymn quoted below are full of comforting reminders that God's almighty power and unchangeable love 'cannot be lost by our unworthiness'. Just to read Newton's enumeration of the offices and works of Jesus on behalf of undeserving sinners is a joy. If you are plagued with doubts concerning your salvation, rather than engaging in further introspection on your own imperfections, pick up your Bible and meditate on the perfections of Jesus Christ!

Assurance is the result of a competent spiritual knowledge of the person and work of Christ as revealed in the gospel, and a consciousness of dependence on him and his work alone for salvation... This knowledge is wrought in us by the [Holy] Spirit, through the medium of the written Word. He teaches no unrevealed truths. We are not to expect that he will assure us as by a voice from heaven, or by a sudden impulse upon our hearts, that our names in particular are written in the book of life; but he opens our understandings to understand the Scripture (Luke 24:45), to assent to it, and feel that we are such sinners as are there described; to see the dignity and sufficiency of Christ Jesus, as God-man, the Mediator; the suitableness of his offices; the value of his atonement and righteousness; and the harmony and glory of the divine attributes, in the adorable methods of redeeming love, which renders it just, righteous, and worthy of God to justify and save the believing sinner (Rom. 3:26).

He likewise gives us to understand the freedom and security of the gospel promises, confirmed by the oath of God, and sealed with the blood of the Son. He shows us the establishment and immutability of the covenant of grace; convinces us that there is a fulness of wisdom, grace, life, and strength, treasured up in Christ, for the use and support of those who in themselves are poor, miserable, and helpless, and to be freely communicated in measure and season as he sees necessary, to support, nourish, and revive the believing soul, and to lead him in the path of perseverance to everlasting life. Such a discovery of almighty power and unchangeable love engaged for the infallible salvation of every believer, which they cannot lose by their unworthiness, nor be deprived of by all the opposition which earth or hell can raise against them (John 10:28-29), produces a suitable assurance in the soul that receives it. And we can confidently say, 'We know we are of God,' when we can in this manner know in whom we have believed.

Such discoveries of the person and grace of Christ are connected with a heartfelt consciousness that the believer's dependence, for all the great hopes and ends of salvation, are fixed on him and his work alone. They draw forth acts of surrender and trust, and keep the mind from forming any vain scheme of hope or refuge, either in whole or in part, from any other quarter... Indeed, from the very first dawnings of faith, as I have observed, the soul is led to commit itself into the hands of Jesus; but while knowledge was weak, and the heart very imperfectly humbled, there was a secret, though unallowed, dependence upon self, upon resolutions, frames [i.e. states of mind], and duties. But as Jesus rises more glorious in the eye of faith, self is in the same degree depressed and renounced; and when we certainly see that there is no safety or stability but in his name, we as certainly feel that we expect them from him, and from him only. And the Holy Spirit assists here likewise, bears a comfortable witness with our spirits (Romans 8:15-16), by drawing us to a throne of grace, pleading in us as a Spirit of adoption, and prompting us to renew the renunciation of ourselves, 'and to glory in Jesus, as made unto us, of God, wisdom, righteousness, sanctification, and redemption' (1 Corinthians 1:30), from day to day. And from hence arises a solid, permanent assurance.

(*Twenty Sermons Preached in the Parish Church of Olney*,
Sermon 20)

Questions to unbelief

*I*f to Jesus for relief
My soul has fled by prayer,
Why should I give way to grief,
Or heart-consuming care?
Are not all things in his hand?
Has he not his promise past?
Will he then regardless stand
And let me sink at last?

While I know his providence
Disposes each event,
Shall I judge by feeble sense,
And yield to discontent?
If he worms and sparrows feed,
Clothe the grass in rich array,
Can he see a child in need,
And turn his eye away?

When his name was quite unknown,
And sin my life employed,
Then he watched me as his own,
Or I had been destroyed:
Now his mercy seat I know,
Now by grace am reconciled;
Would he spare me while a foe,
To leave me when a child?

If he all my wants supplied
When I disdained to pray,
Now his Spirit is my guide,
How can he say me nay?
If he would not give me up,
When my soul against him fought,

Will he disappoint the hope
Which he himself has wrought?

If he shed his precious blood
To bring me to his fold,
Can I think that meaner [i.e. lesser] good
He ever will withhold?
Satan, vain is thy device!
Here my hope rests well-assured;
In that great redemption-price,
I see the whole secured.

(*Olney Hymns,* Book 3, Hymn 38)

S uggested Scripture readings: John 10:12-30; Romans 8:31-39

'We know that we are of God' (I John 5:19).

On his promise I rely

Below are some extracts from tender pastoral letters which Newton penned in response to those who wrote to him with questions about the doctrine of final perseverance (often referred to today as the doctrine of eternal security). How these wise and comforting words must have bolstered the confidence and strengthened the hope of these struggling believers!

To be at an uncertainty in a point of so great importance, to have nothing to trust to for our continuance in well-doing, but our own feeble efforts, our partial diligence and short-sighted care, must surely be distressing if we rightly consider how unable we are in ourselves to withstand the forces of the world, the flesh, and the devil, which are combined against our peace... [A believer's confidence is based on] the unchangeableness of God, the intercession of Christ, the union which subsists between him and his people...

Upon these grounds, my friend, why may not you, who have fled for refuge to the hope set before you, and committed your soul to Jesus, rejoice in his salvation, and say, 'While Christ is the foundation, root, head, and husband of his people, while the Word of God is Yea and Amen, while the counsels of God are unchangeable, while we have a Mediator and High Priest before the throne, while the Holy Spirit is willing and able to bear witness to the truths of the gospel, while God is wiser than men, and stronger than Satan — so long the believer in Jesus is and shall be safe'? ...

We cannot watch, unless he watches with us; we cannot strive, unless he strives with us; we cannot stand one moment, unless he holds us up; and we believe we must perish after all, unless his faithfulness is engaged to keep us.

(*Forty-One Letters on Religious Subjects*, Letter 9)

I shall only say, the belief of [the doctrine of final perseverance] is essential to my peace. I cannot take upon me to judge the hearts and feelings of others; but from the knowledge I have of my own, I am reduced by necessity to take refuge in a hope which, through mercy, I find strongly encouraged in the Scripture, that Jesus, to whom I have been led to commit myself, has engaged to save me absolutely, and from first to last. I think he has promised not only that he will not depart from me, but that he will put, keep, and maintain his fear in my heart, that I shall not depart from him: and if he does not, I have no security against my turning apostate. For I am so weak, inconsistent, and sinful, so encompassed with snares, and liable to such assaults from the subtlety, vigilance, and power of Satan, that, unless I am 'kept by the power of God through faith' [1 Peter 1:5], I am sure I cannot endure to the end. I believe the Lord will keep me while I walk humbly and obediently before him; but were this all, it would be cold comfort. I am prone to wander, and need a Shepherd whose watchful eye, compassionate heart, and boundless mercy will pity, pardon, and restore my backslidings. For though, by his goodness and not my own, I have hitherto been preserved from dishonouring my profession [i.e. of faith in Christ] in the sight of men; yet I feel those evils within, which would presently break loose and bear me down from bad to worse, were he not ever present with me to control them. And therefore I conclude, they who comfortably hope to see his face in glory, but depend in whole or in part upon their own watchfulness and endeavours to preserve themselves from falling, must either be much wiser, better and stronger than I am, or at least cannot have so deep and painful a sense of their own weakness and vileness as daily experience forces upon me. I desire to be found in the use of the Lord's appointed means for the renewal of my strength, but I dare not undertake to watch a single hour, nor do I find sufficiency to think a good thought, nor a power in myself of resisting any temptation.

My strength is perfect weakness
And all I have is sin.

In short, I must sit down in despair, if I did not believe (the apostle, I think, allows me to be confident) that he who has begun a good work in me will perform it until the day of Jesus Christ [Philippians 1:6].

> (*Letters intended for a Sequel to Cardiphonia*,
> 'To the Rev. Dr ...,' Letter 11)

Would you have assurance? ... Assurance grows by repeated conflict, by our repeated experimental proof [i.e. proof based on experience] of the Lord's power and goodness to save; when we have been brought very low indeed and helped, sorely wounded and healed, cast down and raised again, have given up all hope, and been suddenly snatched from danger, and placed in safety; and when these things have been repeated in us a thousand times over, we begin to learn to trust simply to the Word and power of God, beyond and against appearances: and this trust, when habitual and strong, bears the name assurance; for even assurance has degrees.

(*Cardiphonia*, 'Seven Letters to Mrs ...', Letter 2)

The following hymn expresses in meter and rhyme the same bold confidence in God's promises to complete the work that he has begun in his children. My favourite couplet says:

Ere he called me, well he knew
What a heart like mine would do.

In the *Olney Hymnal* there is a footnote attached to these lines citing Isaiah 48:8, which states that the Lord '... knew that you [Israel] would deal very treacherously; and you have been called a rebel from birth'. I find such comfort in this reminder that, while I continue to be discouraged, and at times even shocked, by my ongoing struggle with sin, God is not surprised by it. He has always known the depths of wickedness in my heart, and yet he has chosen to love me, forgive me and, one day, will fully perfect me.

Confidence

Yes! Since God himself has said it,
  On the promise I rely;
His good word demands my credit;
What can unbelief reply?
He is strong and can fulfil;
He is truth and therefore will.

As to all the doubts and questions,
Which my spirit often grieve,

These are Satan's sly suggestions,
And I need no answer give;
He would fain destroy my hope,
But the promise bears it up.

Sure, the Lord thus far has brought me
By his watchful tender care;
Sure, 'tis he himself has taught me
How to seek his face by prayer.
After so much mercy past,
Will he give me up at last?

True, I've been a foolish creature,
And have sinned against his grace;
But forgiveness is his nature,
Though he justly hides his face;
Ere he called me, well he knew
What a heart like mine would do.

In my Saviour's intercession
Therefore I will still confide;
Lord, accept my free confession,
I have sinned, but thou hast died;
This is all I have to plead;
This is all the plea I need.

(Olney Hymns, Book 3, Hymn 52)

Suggested Scripture readings: Luke 14:28-30; Hebrews 7:25; Romans 8:34-39; John 14:14-19; 15:1-2

'For I am confident of this very thing, that he who began a good work in you will perfect it until the day of Christ Jesus' (Phil. 1:6).

The enemies of assurance

Newton ministered in an age in which there was no small controversy about whether salvation, once gained, could be lost. There
were certainly preachers and movements who could be held
responsible for denying the plain, biblical doctrine of final perseverance. However, in the following excerpts, Newton asserts that the
real enemies that keep men from the joy of complete assurance in a
faith that will continue to the end are found within men's own
hearts!

Insincerity

Where grace is really implanted by the Holy Spirit, it will
surely prevail at length, and subdue the whole soul to the
obedience of faith. But in too many there is for a long time
not only great opposition from indwelling corruption, but a
secret cleaving of the will to evil. A double-mindedness
[James 1:8], a kind of halting between two opinions... A
habitual indulgence of known or suspected evil, or a habitual neglect of any known duty, will certainly prevent the
growth of grace and consolation. For the Lord claims (what
is his just due) the whole heart, and will not afford the
strengthening light of his countenance, while any idol is
deliberately set up in his presence... Till the pride and
naughtiness of our spirits are conquered, and we are made
willing to give up all, to renounce whatever is contrary to
his precepts ... it is vain to expect a full and abiding assurance of his love.

Indolence

With respect to this valuable blessing, it may often be said,
'Ye receive not, because ye ask not' [James 4:2]. It is too
common for those who were earnest in crying for mercy,
while they thought themselves under the curse and power
of the law, to grow slack and remiss in prayer soon after

they obtain some hope of salvation from the gospel; and particularly they do not 'give all diligence to make their calling and election sure' [2 Peter 1:10], in the careful use of every means appointed for their establishment in the truth as it is in Christ Jesus... They go on for months or years in a complaining, unsettled state; and deservedly, because they are not earnest in seeking, asking, waiting, knocking at the gate of wisdom, and at the throne of grace, for that blessing which the Lord has promised to those who persevere in wrestling prayer, and will take no denial.

Misapprehensions [i.e. Misunderstandings]

These arise from a neglect of examining the Scriptures, and in undue deference to the decisions of men. [1] If assurance is supposed unattainable, it will consequently not be sought after. [2] If it is expected as an instantaneous impression of the Spirit of God upon the mind, independent of his Word, or to arise from some sudden powerful application of a particular text of Scripture, this persuasion will end in disappointment... Those who depend chiefly upon such impressions, instead of endeavouring to grow in the scriptural knowledge of Christ, are generally as changeable in their hopes as in their frame [of mind]. [3] If inherent sanctification, or a considerable increase of it, is considered as the proper ground of assurance, those who are most humble, sincere, and desirous of being conformed to the will of God will be the most perplexed and discouraged in their search after it... These mistakes ... prevent many from seeking after assurance at all, and bewilder many more, by putting them on a wrong pursuit.

(*Twenty Sermons Preached in the Parish Church of Olney,*
Sermon 20)

Unbelief is the primary cause of all inquietude, from the moment that our hearts are drawn to seek salvation by

Jesus. The inability to take God at his word should not merely be lamented as an infirmity, but watched, and prayed, and fought against as a great sin... It often deceives us under the guise of humility, as though it would be presumptuous, in such sinners as we are, to believe the declarations of the God of truth... But this is an affront to the wisdom and goodness of God, who points out to us the Son of his love, as our wisdom, righteousness, sanctification, and redemption, without any regard to what we have been, or to what we are, excepting that broken and contrite spirit which only himself can create in us.

(*Miscellaneous papers extracted from periodical publications*, 'Thoughts on Faith and the Assurance of Faith')

S uggested Scripture readings: Proverbs 2:1-7; 2 Peter 1:5-11

> '*Test yourselves to see if you are in the faith; examine yourselves!*' (2 Cor. 13:5).

2.

GROWING IN HOLINESS

Strange and mysterious is my life;
What opposites I feel within!
A stable peace, a constant strife,
The rule of grace, the power of sin:
Too often I am captive led,
Yet daily triumph in my Head.

The Old Vicarage, Olney, from the churchyard.
The dormer window on the far right looks out from John Newton's study,
where he wrote many of the letters and hymns quoted in this book.

Progressive sanctification

Grace in the blade

It was while Newton held the post of Surveyor of the Tides (a customs official) at the busy international port of Liverpool that he became acquainted with John Wesley. There he heard Wesley preach as often as the itinerant preacher's ministry brought him to that area. In time, the two became acquainted with one another. Newton developed a respect for Wesley, who was twenty-two years his senior, and through correspondence discussed with him his own growing desires to be a preacher of the gospel. Their rapport developed into friendship and the two exchanged letters frequently. Newton was a pall-bearer at the funeral of John's brother Charles Wesley, another great hymn-writer.

But while Newton agreed with Wesley concerning the doctrines of original sin, justification by faith and holiness, he also saw weaknesses in his friend's theology. He particularly took issue with Wesley's teaching on perfectionism, which claimed that a Christian could reach a state of 'instantaneous and entire sanctification' in which the person no longer sinned. While Newton's and Wesley's differing views over the doctrines of predestination, the extent of the atonement and final perseverance had never caused a significant strain in their relationship, Newton considered Wesley's views on perfectionism so dangerous to the church that eventually their friendship cooled. He wrote to Wesley, 'But with respect to Perfection, I confess that I am not so indifferent. I should think it my duty to oppose it (if it had any prevalence in these parts) with my whole strength, not as an opinion, but as a dangerous mistake, which appears to me subversive of the very foundations of Christian experience — and which has in fact given occasion to the most grievous offences, and the wildest sallies of Enthusiasm [i.e. fanaticism].'[1]

Newton described a minister who held perfectionist views as 'one of the most disagreeable persons I ever met... He pretended [i.e. laid claim] to sinless perfection, and supposing he ought to make good his claim by something extraordinary, he maintained the most disgusting affectation, labouring to set himself off [i.e. show himself to advantage] in everything he did or said.'[2] Newton further documented his strong opposition to this doctrine in a letter in which he stated: 'I account it a part of the happiness of my present situation that Mr Wesley has no society here [at Olney], nor for half a score [i.e. ten] miles around me.'[3]

Given Newton's grave concern about the harmful results of the popular teaching on perfectionism, it is little wonder that so many of his letters, sermons and hymns deal with the believer's lifelong battle with remaining sin and the progressive, *not* instantaneous, nature of God's sanctifying work in the soul. So much in Newton's writings reflects the sentiments of William Grimshaw, a respected colleague of Newton's who stated, 'My perfection is to see my own imperfection.'[4]

Newton wrote three letters addressing what he saw as the three typical stages of spiritual growth in the life of a believer. Taking his imagery from Jesus' words in Mark 4:28 (AV), he entitled these letters 'Grace in the Blade', 'Grace in the Ear' and 'The Full Corn in the Ear'. Interlaced with these letters are hymns on the same themes.

> According to your desire, I sit down to give you my general views of a progressive work of grace, in the several stages of a believer's experience; which I shall mark by the different characters, 'A', 'B', 'C', answerable to the distinctions which our Lord teaches us to observe from the growth of the corn (Mark 4:28)...
>
> By 'A', I would understand a person who is under the drawings of God, which will infallibly lead him to the Lord Jesus Christ for life and salvation...

He receives grace from Jesus, whereby he is enabled to fight against sin: his conscience is tender; his troubles are chiefly spiritual troubles; and he thinks, if he could attain a sure and abiding sense of his acceptance in the Beloved, hardly any outward trial would be capable of giving him much disturbance. Indeed, notwithstanding the weakness of his faith, and the prevalence of a legal [i.e. legalistic] spirit, which greatly hurts him, there are some things in his present experience which he may, perhaps, look back upon with regret hereafter, when his hope and knowledge will be more established; particularly that sensibility and keenness of appetite with which he now attends the ordinances, desiring the sincere milk of the word with earnestness and eagerness, as a babe does the breast. He counts the hours from one opportunity to another; and the attention and desire with which he hears may be read in his countenance. His zeal is ... lively; and may be, for want of experience, too importunate and forward. He has a love for souls and a concern for the glory of God, which, though it may at some times create him trouble, and at others be mixed with some undue motions of self, yet in its principle is highly desirable and commendable (John 18:10).

The grace of God influences both the understanding and the affections. Warm affections, without knowledge, can rise no higher than superstition; and that knowledge which does not influence the heart and affections will only make a hypocrite. The true believer is rewarded in both respects; yet we may observe that, though 'A' is not without knowledge, this state is more usually remarkable for the warmth and liveliness of the affections. On the other hand, as the work advances, though the affections are not left out, yet it seems to be carried on principally in the understanding. The old Christian has more solid, judicious, connected views of the Lord Jesus Christ, and the glories of his person and redeeming love: hence his hope is more established, his dependence more simple, and his peace and strength ... more abiding and uniform than in the case of the young convert; but the latter has, for the most part, the advantage in point of sensible [i.e. readily perceived] fervency. A tree is most valuable when laden with ripe fruit, but it has a peculiar [i.e. particular] beauty when in blossom. It is springtime with 'A'; he is in bloom, and, by the grace and blessing of the heavenly Husbandman [i.e. Vinedresser], will bear fruit in old age. His faith is weak, but his heart is warm... The very desire and bent of his soul is to God, and to the word of his grace. His knowledge is but small, but it is growing every day. If he is not a 'father' or a 'young man' in grace, he is a dear 'child'. The Lord has visited his heart, delivered him from the love of sin, and fixed his desires supremely upon Jesus Christ...

(*Twenty-Six Letters on Religious Subjects*, Letter 10)

Suggested Scripture readings: 2 Corinthians 3:18; 1 Peter 2:1-3; 2 Peter 3:18

'The earth produces by itself, first the blade, then the ear, then the full grain in the ear' (Mark 4:28, ESV).

Grace in the ear

I have already attempted ... a general delineation of a young convert, under the character of 'A', and am now to speak of him by the name of 'B'.

Now [that] faith is stronger, it has more to grapple with. I think the characteristic state of 'A' is desire, and of 'B' is conflict... So there are usually trials and exercises in 'B's' experience, something different in their kind, and sharper in their measure, than what 'A' was exposed to, or indeed had strength to endure. 'A', like Israel, has been delivered from Egypt by great power and a stretched-out arm, has been pursued and terrified by many enemies, has given himself up for lost again and again. He has at last seen his enemies destroyed, and has sung the song of Moses and the Lamb upon the banks of the Red Sea. Then he commences 'B'. Perhaps, like Israel, he thinks his difficulties are at an end, and expects to go on rejoicing till he enters the promised land. But, alas! his difficulties are in a manner but beginning; he has a wilderness before him, of which he is not aware. The Lord is now about to suit his dispensations [i.e. arrange his circumstances] to humble and to prove him, and to show him what is in his heart, that he may do him good at the latter end, and that all the glory may redound to his own free grace…

'B' is not all spirit. A depraved nature still cleaves to him, and he has the seeds of every natural corruption yet remaining in his heart. He lives likewise in a world that is full of snares and occasions suited to draw forth those corruptions; and he is surrounded by invisible spiritual enemies, the extent of whose power and subtlety he is yet to learn by painful experience. 'B' knows, in general, the nature of his Christian warfare, and sees his right to live upon Jesus for righteousness and strength. He is not unwilling to endure hardships as a good soldier of Jesus Christ, and believes that, though he may be sore thrust at that he may fall, the Lord will be his stay. He knows that his heart is 'deceitful and desperately wicked'; but he does not, he cannot know at first, the full meaning of that expression. Yet it is for the Lord's glory, and will in the end make his grace and love still more precious, that 'B' should find new and mortifying proofs of an evil nature as he goes on, such as he could not once have believed had they been foretold to him, as in the case of Peter (Mark 14:29). And in effect, the abominations of

the heart do not appear in their full strength and aggravation
... [except to one who] has tasted that the Lord is gracious,
and rejoiced in his salvation. The exceeding sinfulness of sin
is manifested, not so much by its breaking through the restraint of threatenings and commands, as by its being capable of acting against light and against love...

I apprehend that, in the state of 'B' — that is, for a season after we have known the Lord — we have usually the
most sensible [i.e. keenly felt] and distressing experience of
our evil natures. I do not say that it is necessary that we
should be left to fall into gross outward sin, in order to
know what is in our hearts... But, oh, the multiplied instances of stupidity, ingratitude, impatience, and rebellion,
to which my conscience has been witness! ... We are prone
to spiritual pride, to self-dependence, to vain confidence, to
creature [i.e. earthly] attachments, and a train of evils. The
Lord often discovers [i.e. reveals] to us one sinful disposition by exposing us to another. By a variety of these exercises, through the overruling and edifying influences of the
Holy Spirit, 'B' is trained up in a growing knowledge of
himself and of the Lord.

(*Twenty-Six Letters on Religious Subjects*, Letter 11)

A sick soul

*P*hysician of my sin-sick soul,
    To thee I bring my case;
My raging malady control
And heal me by thy grace.

Pity the anguish I endure,
See how I mourn and pine;
For never can I hope a cure
From any hand but thine.

I would disclose my whole complaint,
But where shall I begin?
No words of mine can fully paint
That worst distemper, sin.

It lies not in a single part,
But through my frame is spread:
A burning fever in my heart,
A palsy in my head.

It makes me deaf, and dumb, and blind,
And impotent, and lame;
And overclouds and fills my mind
With folly, fear, and shame.

A thousand evil thoughts intrude
Tumultuous in my breast,
Which indispose me for my food,
And rob me of my rest.

Lord, I am sick; regard my cry,
And set my spirit free!
Say, canst thou let a sinner die,
Who longs to live to thee?

(Olney Hymns, Book 1, Hymn 83)

Self-acquaintance

*D*ear Lord, accept a sinful heart,
     Which of itself complains
And mourns, with much and frequent smart,
The evil it contains.

There fiery seeds of anger lurk,
Which often hurt my frame;

And wait but for the tempter's work,
To fan them to a flame.

Legality holds out a bribe
To purchase life from thee;
And discontent would fain prescribe
How thou shalt deal with me.

While unbelief withstands thy grace,
And puts the mercy by;
Presumption, with a brow of brass,
Says, 'Give me, or I die.'

How eager are my thoughts to roam
In quest of what they love!
But, ah! when duty calls them home,
How heavily they move!

Oh, cleanse me in a Saviour's blood,
Transform me by thy power,
And make me thy beloved abode,
And let me rove no more.

(*Olney Hymns*, Book 3, Hymn 26)

The way of access

O ne glance of thine, eternal Lord,
   Pierces all nature through;
Nor heaven, nor earth, nor hell, afford
A shelter from thy view!

The mighty whole, each smaller part,
At once before thee lies;
And every thought, of every heart,
Is open to thine eyes.

Though greatly from myself concealed,
Thou seest my inward frame;
To thee I always stand revealed,
Exactly as I am.

Since therefore I can hardly bear
What in myself I see;
How vile and black must I appear,
Most holy God, to thee!

But since my Saviour stands between,
In garments dyed in blood;
'Tis he, instead of me, is seen,
When I approach to God.

Thus, though a sinner, I am safe;
He pleads before the throne,
His life and death, in my behalf,
And calls my sins his own.

What wondrous love, what mysteries,
In this appointment shine!
My breaches of the law are his,
And his obedience mine.

(*Olney Hymns*, Book 3, Hymn 41)

S uggested Scripture readings: Psalm 139:23-24; Mark 14:26-31; Romans 7:15-25

'For I know that nothing good dwells in me, that is, in my flesh; for the willing is present in me, but the doing of the good is not' (Rom. 7:18).

Grace in the full corn

By way of distinction, I assigned to 'A' the characteristic of *desire*, to 'B' that of *conflict*. I can think of no single word more descriptive of the state of 'C' than *contemplation...*

'C's' happiness and superiority to 'B' lies chiefly in this, that, by the Lord's blessings on the use of means — such as prayer, reading, and hearing of the Word, and by a sanctified improvement of what he has seen of the Lord, and of his own heart, in the course of his experience — he has attained clearer, deeper, and more comprehensive views of the mystery of redeeming love; of the glorious excellency of the Lord Jesus, in his person, offices, grace, and faithfulness; of the harmony and glory of all the divine perfections manifested in and by him to the church; of the stability, beauty, fulness, and certainty of the Holy Scriptures, and of the heights, depths, lengths, and breadths of the love of God in Christ. Thus, though his sensible [i.e. conscious] feelings may not be so warm as when he was in the state of 'A', his judgement is more solid, his mind more fixed, his thoughts more habitually exercised upon the things within the veil. His great business is to behold the glory of God in Christ; and by beholding, he is changed into the same image, and brings forth in an imminent and uniform manner the fruits of righteousness, which are by Jesus Christ to the glory and praise of God. His contemplations are not barren speculations, but have a real influence, and enable him to exemplify the Christian character to more advantage, and with more consistence, than can in the present state of things be expected either from 'A' or 'B'. The following particulars may illustrate my meaning.

1. *Humility.* A measure of this grace is to be expected in every true Christian; but it can only appear in proportion to

the knowledge they have of Christ and of their own hearts. It is a part of 'C's' daily employment to look back upon the way by which the Lord has led him; and while he reviews the Ebenezers [i.e. monuments to the faithfulness of God] he has set up all along the road, he sees, in an almost equal number, the monuments of his own perverse returns, and how he has in a thousand instances rendered to the Lord evil for good. Comparing these things together, he can without affectation adopt the apostle's language and style [i.e. call] himself 'less than the least of all saints, and of sinners the chief'. 'A' and 'B' know that they ought to be humbled; but 'C' is truly so...

2. *Spirituality.* A spiritual taste, and disposition to account all things mean and vain, in comparison of the knowledge and love of God in Christ, are essential to a true Christian. The world can never be his prevailing choice (1 John 2:15). Yet we are ... prone to an undue attachment to worldly things. I believe the Lord seldom gives his people a considerable victory over this evil principle until he has let them feel how deeply it is rooted in their hearts... A considerable part of our trials are mercifully appointed to wean us from this propensity; and it is gradually weakened by the Lord's showing us at one time the vanity of the creature, and at another his own excellence and all-sufficiency. Even 'C' is not perfect in this respect; but he is more sensible [i.e. aware] of the evil of such attachments, more humbled for them, more watchful against them, and more delivered from them. He still feels a fetter, but he longs to be free...

3. *A union of the heart to the glory and will of God* is another noble distinction of 'C's' spirit. The glory of God and the good of his people are inseparably connected. But of these great ends, the first is unspeakably the highest and the most important, and [that] into which everything else will be

finally resolved. Now, in proportion as we advance nearer
to him, our judgement, aim, and end will be conformable to
his, and his glory will have the highest place in our hearts.
At first it is not so, or but very imperfectly. Our concern is
chiefly about ourselves; nor can it be otherwise. The convinced soul enquires, 'What shall I do to be saved?' The
young convert is intent upon sensible [i.e. creature] comforts... But 'C' has attained to more enlarged views; he has
a desire to depart and to be with Christ, which would be
importunate if he considered only himself; but his chief
desire is that God may be glorified in him, whether by his
life or by his death. He is not his own; nor does he desire to
be his own; but so that the power of Jesus may be manifested in him, he will take pleasure in infirmities, in distresses, in temptations; and though he longs for heaven,
would be content to live as long as Methuselah upon earth,
if, by anything he could do or suffer, the will and glory of
God might be promoted... And though he loves and adores
the Lord for what he has done and suffered for him, delivered him from, and appointed him to, yet he loves and
adores him likewise with a more simple and direct love, in
which self is in a manner forgot, from the consideration of
his glorious excellence and perfections, as he is in himself.
That God in Christ is glorious over all, and blessed for ever,
is the very joy of his soul; and his heart can frame no higher
wish than that the sovereign, wise, holy will of God may be
accomplished in him, and all his creatures. Upon this grand
principle his prayers, schemes, and actions are formed.
Thus 'C' is already made like the angels; and, so far as is
consistent with the inseparable remnants of a fallen nature,
the will of God is regarded by him upon earth as it is by the
inhabitants of heaven.

(*Forty-one Letters on Religious Subjects*, Letter 12)

*S*uggested Scripture readings: Matthew 5:16; John 15:8; Ephesians 1:3-14; 1 Peter 4:10-11

> *'... that we who were the first to hope in Christ would be to the praise of his glory'* (Eph. 1:12).

Battling remaining sin

I would not ... yet I ...

The excerpts quoted below are based on Newton's meditations on Romans 7:14-25, which speaks of the chasm between the apostle Paul's spiritual desires and his actual practice. In the following letter, Newton expresses a similar experience with a series of 'I would not ... yet I ...' statements. As I read this letter and the hymns that follow, I was once again staggered by Newton's humble honesty. I have never heard anyone else address (as he does in the final paragraph of the letter) the disturbing truth that, even in striving against sin, the heart is corrupt.

I would not be the sport and prey of wild, vain, foolish, and worse imagination; but this evil is present with me. My heart is like a highway, like a city without walls or gates... [Sinful thoughts] can obtain access ... at any time, or in any place: neither the study, the pulpit, or even the Lord's Table, exempt me from their intrusion. I sometimes compare my *words* to the treble of an instrument, which my *thoughts* accompany with a kind of bass ... in which every rule of harmony is broken, every possible combination of discord and confusion is introduced, utterly inconsistent with, and contradictory to, the intended melody...

I find something within me which cherishes and cleaves to those evils from which I ought to start and flee as I should if a toad or a serpent was put in my food, or in my bed... Surely he who finds himself capable of this may ... subscribe himself [i.e. describe himself as] less than the least of all saints, and of sinners the very chief.

I would not be influenced by a principle of self on any occasion; yet this evil I often do... The pride of others often offends me, and makes me studious to hide my own; because their good opinion of me depends much upon their not perceiving it. But the Lord knows how this dead fly taints and spoils my best services...

I would not indulge vain reasonings concerning the counsels, ways, and providences of God; yet I am prone to do it. That the Judge of all the earth will do right is to me as evident and necessary as that two and two make four. I believe that he has a sovereign right to do what he will with his own, and that this sovereignty is but another name for the unlimited exercise of wisdom and goodness. But my reasonings are often such as if I had never heard of these principles, or had formally renounced them...

I would not cleave to a covenant of works [i.e. try to earn salvation by my own works]: it should seem from the foregoing particulars, and many others which I could mention, that I have reasons enough to deter me from this. Yet even this I do... I am invited to take the water of life *freely*, yet often discouraged, because I have nothing wherewith to pay for it. If I am at times favoured with some liberty from the above-mentioned evils, it rather gives me a more favourable opinion of myself than increases my admiration of the Lord's goodness to so unworthy a creature; and when the returning tide of my corruptions convinces me that *I am still the same* ... I feel a weariness of being beholden to [the Lord] for such continued multiplied forgiveness; and I fear that some part of my striving against sin, and my desires after an increase of sanctification, arises from a secret wish that I might not be so absolutely and entirely indebted to him.

(*Cardiphonia*, 'Twenty-Six Letters to a Nobleman', Letter 5)

The good that I would I do not
Romans 7:19

I would, but cannot, sing;
Guilt has untuned my voice;
The serpent sin's envenomed sting
Has poisoned all my joys.

I know the Lord is nigh,
And would, but cannot, pray;
For Satan meets me when I try,
And frights my soul away.

I would, but can't, repent
Though I endeavour oft;
This stony heart can ne'er relent
Till Jesus make it soft.

I would, but cannot, love,
Though wooed by love divine;
No arguments have power to move
A soul so base as mine.

I would, but cannot, rest
In God's most holy will;
I know what he appoints is best,
Yet murmur at it still!

Oh, could I but believe!
Then all would easy be;
I would, but cannot; Lord, relieve!
My help must come from thee!

But if indeed I would,
Though I can nothing do,
Yet the desire is something good,
For which my praise is due.

By nature prone to ill,
Till thine appointed hour,
I was as destitute of will,
As now I am of power.

Wilt thou not crown, at length,
The work thou hast begun,
And with a will, afford me strength
In all thy ways to run?

(Olney Hymns, Book 1, Hymn 126)

Suggested **Scripture** **readings**: Romans 7:14-25; Galatians 5:16-26

'For the good that I want, I do not do, but I practise the very evil that I do not want' (Rom. 7:19).

What a contradiction!

When it comes to growing in holiness, who is responsible — you, or God? The Bible teaches that the answer to that question is 'Both'. Newton was careful to offer this balanced view of the doctrine of sanctification. On the one hand, he acknowledges that, due to the extent of our depravity and spiritual weakness, we are utterly unable to accomplish any spiritual work on our own; on the other hand, he reminds us of the sizeable list of New Testament imperatives regarding our responsibility to work actively and diligently at ridding our lives of sin.

In the letter below, Newton addresses the undeniable gap between what believers profess to be true with their mouths and what they actually practise in their lives, and attempts to answer the age-old question as to why God allows believers to battle against indwelling sin rather than simply eradicating it from their lives at conversion.

What a contradiction is a believer to himself! He is called a 'believer' emphatically because he cordially assents to the Word of God; but, alas! how often unworthy of the name! If I was to describe him from the Scripture character, I should say he is one whose heart is athirst for God, for his glory, his image, his presence; his affections are fixed upon an unseen Saviour; his treasures, and consequently his thoughts, are on high, beyond the bounds of sense. Having experienced much forgiveness, he is full of bowels [i.e. deep feelings] of mercy to all around, and having been often deceived by his own heart, he dares trust it no more, but lives by faith in the Son of God, for wisdom, righteousness, and sanctification, and derives from him grace for grace; sensible [i.e. conscious] that without him he has not sufficiency even to think a good thought. In short — he is dead to the world, to sin, to self, but alive to God, and lively in his service. Prayer is his breath, the Word of God his food, and the ordinances more precious to him than the light of the sun. Such is a believer — in his judgement and prevailing desires.

But was I to describe him from experience, especially at some times, how different would the picture be! Though he knows that communion with God is his highest privilege, he too seldom finds it so; on the contrary, if duty, conscience, and necessity did not compel, he would leave the throne of grace unvisited from day to day. He takes up the Bible, conscious that it is the fountain of life and true comfort; yet perhaps, while he is making the reflection, he feels a secret distaste which prompts him to lay it down, and give his preference to a newspaper. He needs not to be told of the vanity and uncertainty of all beneath the sun; and yet is almost as much elated or cast down by a trifle as those who have their portion in this world. He believes that all things shall work together for his good, and that the Most High God appoints, adjusts, and overrules all his concerns; yet he feels the risings of fear, anxiety, and displeasure, as though the contrary was true. He owns himself ignorant, and liable to be deceived by a thousand fallacies; yet is easily betrayed into positiveness [i.e. a dogmatic attitude] and self-conceit. He feels himself an unprofitable, unfaithful, unthankful servant, and therefore blushes to harbour a thought of desiring the esteem and commendations of men, yet he cannot suppress it...

How can these things be, or why are they permitted? Since the Lord hates sin, teaches his people to hate it and cry against it, and has promised to hear their prayers, how is it that they go thus burdened [i.e. that they carry such a burden]? ... By these exercises he teaches us more truly to know and feel the utter depravity and corruption of our whole nature, that we are indeed defiled in every part. His method of salvation is likewise hereby exceedingly endeared to us: we see that it is and must be of grace, wholly of grace; and that the Lord Jesus Christ, and his perfect righteousness, is and must be our all in all. His power likewise, in maintaining his own work, notwithstanding our infirmities, temptations, and enemies, is hereby displayed in the clearest light; his strength is manifested in our weakness. Satan likewise is more remarkably disappointed and put to shame, when he finds bounds set to his rage and policy, beyond which he cannot pass; and that those in whom he finds so much to work upon, and over whom he so often prevails for a season, escape at last out of his hands... Further, by what believers feel in themselves they learn by degrees how to warn, pity, and bear with others. A soft, patient, and compassionate spirit, and a readiness and skill in comforting those who are cast down, is not perhaps attainable in any other way. And, lastly, I believe nothing more habitually reconciles a child of God to the thought of death than the wearisomeness of this warfare. Death is unwelcome to nature — but then, and not till then, the conflict will cease. Then we shall sin no more. The flesh, with all its attendant evils, will be laid in the grave. Then the soul, which has been partaker of a new and heavenly birth, shall be freed from every incumbrance, and stand perfect in the Redeemer's righteousness before God in glory.

But though these evils cannot be wholly removed, it is worthwhile to enquire, secondly, how they might be mitigated. This we are encouraged to hope for. The Word of God directs and animates to a growth in grace; and though we can do nothing spiritually of ourselves, yet there is a part assigned us. We cannot conquer the obstacles in our way by our own strength; yet we *can* give way to them; and if we do, it is our sin, and will be our sorrow… The apostles exhort us to give all diligence, to resist the devil, to purge ourselves from all filthiness of the flesh and spirit; to give ourselves to reading, meditation, and prayer; to watch, to put on the whole armour of God, and to abstain from all appearance of evil. Faithfulness to light received, and a sincere endeavour to conform to the means prescribed in the Word of God, with an humble application to the blood of sprinkling and the promised Spirit, will undoubtedly be answered by increasing measures of light, faith, strength, and comfort; and we shall know if we follow on to know the Lord.

(*Cardiphonia*, 'Twenty-six Letters to a Nobleman', Letter 2)

S uggested Scripture readings: Philippians 2:12-18; 1 Peter 1:13-16

> 'Work out your salvation with fear and trembling; for it is God who is at work in you' (Phil. 2:12-13).

Defining a Christian

In this letter, Newton comforts a Christian woman who is extremely grieved by the sin that she observes in her own life. Newton expresses his fear that she has been exposed to the harmful teaching of perfectionism, which was continuing to make inroads into the evangelical landscape. The idea of achieving sinless perfection this side of heaven has plagued the church of Christ throughout many generations, leaving in its wake many confused and disillusioned believers. I almost wish that it were true! The idea of never sinning again, never grieving the heart of my God, never hurting those around me, is enormously attractive, but unfortunately utterly contrary to both the plain teaching of Scripture and my own experience. Newton comforts this discouraged believer and reminds her that a struggle with indwelling sin is not only normal, but that Scripture teaches that it is actually a defining characteristic of a Christian.

I am ready to think that some of the sentiments in your letters are not properly yours, such as you yourself have derived from the Scriptures, but rather borrowed from authors or preachers, whose judgement your humility has led you to prefer to your own. At least, I am sure the Scripture does not authorize the conclusion which distresses you, that if you were a child of God you should not feel such changes and oppositions.

Were I to define a Christian, or rather to describe him at large, I know no text I would choose sooner as a ground for the subject than Galatians 5:17 ['For the flesh sets its desire against the Spirit, and the Spirit against the flesh; for these are in opposition to one another, so that you may not do the things that you please']. A Christian has noble aims, which distinguish him from the bulk of mankind. His leading principles, motives, and desires are all supernatural and divine. Could he do as he would, there is not a spirit before the throne [that] should excel him in holiness, love,

and obedience. He would tread in the very footsteps of his
Saviour, fill up every moment in his service, and employ
every breath in his praise. This he would do; but, alas! he
cannot. Against this desire of the spirit, there is a contrary
desire and working of a corrupt nature, which meets him at
every turn. He has a beautiful copy set before him: he is en-
amoured with it, and though he does not expect to equal it,
he writes carefully after it, and longs to attain to the nearest
possible imitation. But indwelling sin and Satan continually jog his hand and spoil his strokes.

You cannot, madam, form a right judgement of yourself,
except you make due allowance for those things which are
not peculiar to yourself, but common to all who have spiritual perception, and are indeed the inseparable appendages
of this mortal state. If it were not so, why should the most
spiritual and gracious people be so ready to confess themselves vile and worthless? One eminent branch of our holiness is a sense of shame and humiliation for those evils
which are only known to ourselves and to him who
searches our hearts, joined with an acquiescence in Jesus,
who is appointed of God, wisdom, righteousness, sanctification, and redemption.

I will venture to assure you that, though you will possess a more stable peace, in proportion as the Lord enables
you to live more simply upon the blood, righteousness, and
grace of the Mediator, you will never grow into a better
opinion of yourself than you have at present. The nearer
you are brought to him, the quicker [i.e. more acute] sense
you will have of your continual need of him, and thereby
your admiration of his power, love, and compassion, will
increase likewise from year to year.

(*Cardiphonia*, 'Three Letters to Mrs G...,' Letter 3)

The inward warfare
Galatians 5:17

Strange and mysterious is my life;
What opposites I feel within!
A stable peace, a constant strife,
The rule of grace, the power of sin:
Too often I am captive led,
Yet daily triumph in my Head.

I prize the privilege of prayer,
But oh, what backwardness to pray!
Though on the Lord I cast my care,
I feel its burden every day:
I seek his will in all I do,
Yet find my own is working too.

I call the promises my own,
And prize them more than mines of gold;
Yet though their sweetness I have known,
They leave me unimpressed and cold:
One hour upon the truth I feed;
The next I know not what I read.

I love the holy day of rest,
When Jesus meets his gathered saints;
Sweet day, of all the week the best!
For its return my spirit pants;
Yet often, through my unbelief,
It proves a day of guilt and grief.

While on my Saviour I rely,
I know my foes shall loose their aim;
And therefore dare their power defy,
Assured of conquest through his name:

But soon my confidence is slain,
And all my fears return again.

Thus different powers within me strive,
And grace, and sin, by turns prevail;
I grieve, rejoice, decline, revive,
And vict'ry hangs in doubtful scale:
But Jesus has his promise passed,
That grace shall overcome at last.

(Olney Hymns, Book 1, Hymn 130)

Suggested **Scripture readings:** Psalm 119:5,20,35,40,133, 176; Galatians 5:16-25

'For the flesh sets its desire against the Spirit, and the Spirit against the flesh; for these are in opposition to one another, so that you may not do the things that you please' (Gal. 5:17).

A leprous house

In these letters, Newton once again addresses the issue of a believer's battle with indwelling sin. With tenderness and disarming honesty, he assures his readers that he speaks 'not from hearsay, but from my own experience'.

The law of sin in my members distresses me; but the gospel yields relief. It is given me to rest in the finished salvation, and to rejoice in Christ Jesus as my all in all. My soul is athirst for nearer and fuller communion with him. Yet he is pleased to keep me short of those sweet consolations in my retired hours which I could desire. However, I cannot doubt but he is with me, and is pleased to keep up in my heart some sense of the evil of sin, the beauty of holiness, my own weakness, and his glorious all-sufficiency. His I am, and him I desire to serve. I am, indeed, a poor servant; but he is a gracious Master. Oh! Who is a God like unto him, that forgiveth iniquity, and casteth the sins of his people into the depths of the sea? I shall not always live thus — the land to which we are going is far different to this wilderness through which he is now leading us. Then we shall see his face, and never, never, sin.

Yet, alas! I must still charge myself with a great want of watchfulness and diligence; the enemy cannot destroy my foundation, but he spreads many nets for my feet, to weaken me, and to interrupt my peace; and, to my shame I must confess, he too often prevails. The Lord in his great mercy preserves me from such sins as would openly dishonour my profession; and a mercy I desire to esteem it, for I can infer from my heart what my life would be, if I were left to myself. I hate sin; I long to be delivered from it, but it is still in me, and works in me. 'Oh, wretched man that I am! Who shall deliver me?' I bless God for Jesus Christ my Lord. To his grace I commend each of you.

Be not surprised that you still find the effects of indwelling sin; it must and will be so. The frame of our fallen nature is depraved throughout, and like a leprous house, it must be entirely demolished, and raised anew. While we are in this world, we shall groan, being burdened. I wish you to long and breathe after a greater measure of sanctification; but we are sometimes betrayed into a legal [i.e. legalistic] spirit, which will make us labour in the very fire to little purpose. If we find deadness and dryness stealing upon us, our only relief is to look to Jesus — to his blood for pardon, to his grace for strength; we can work nothing out of ourselves. To pore over our evils will not cure them; but he who was typified by the brazen serpent is ever present, lifted up to our view in the camp; and one believing sight of him will do more to restore peace to the conscience, and life to our graces, than all our lamentations and resolutions...

Two things we should always guard and pray against: that the knowledge of our acceptance in the Beloved may not make us secure and careless; and likewise, that our endeavours after conformity to his revealed will may not subject us to a spirit of bondage... If I may speak from my own experience, I find that to keep my eye simply upon Christ, as my peace, and my life, is by far the hardest part of my calling. Through mercy, he enables me to avoid what is wrong in the sight of men, but it seems easier to deny self in a thousand instances of outward conduct, than in its ceaseless endeavours to act as a principle of righteousness and power.

John Bunyan, in his advanced years, took notice of the abominations that had still too much place in his heart; one of them was a secret cleavage to the covenant of works [a temptation to attempt to contribute some good works to his salvation]. I am sure this is no small abomination in a believer; but, alas! it cleaves as close to me as my skin, and costs me many a sigh.

(*Letters Intended as a Sequel to Cardiphonia*, 'Eighteen Letters to Several Ladies,' Letters 6, 16, 13)

It is interesting to note Newton's allusion to John Bunyan, who preached a hundred years earlier in Bedford, just a few miles from Olney. Bunyan wrote over sixty books, including *The Pilgrim's Progress*, one of Newton's favourites. Indeed, Newton wrote the preface to, and contributed to the notes of, the 1776 edition. He frequently read aloud from it to those who gathered for the Tuesday prayer meetings in Olney. Bunyan's autobiography, *Grace Abounding to the Chief of Sinners*, contains many of the same honest confessions of struggles with indwelling sin, suggesting that he may have had a strong influence on Newton's views on sanctification.

Every year, and indeed every day, affords me new proofs of the evil and deceitfulness of my heart, and my utter insufficiency to think even a good thought of myself. But I trust, in the course of various exercises, I have been taught more of the power, grace, and all-sufficiency of Jesus. I can commend him to others, not from hearsay, but from my own experience. His name is precious; his love is wonderful; his compassions are boundless. I trust I am enabled to choose him as my all, my Lord, my Strength, my Saviour, my Portion. I long for more grace to love him better; for, alas! I have reason to number myself among the least of saints and the chief of sinners.

(*Letters Intended as a Sequel to Cardiphonia,* 'Eighteen Letters to Several Ladies,' Letter 18)

The poor believer, however blameless and exemplary in the sight of men, appears in his own view the most inconsistent character under the sun. He can hardly think it is so with others and, judging of *them* by what he *sees*, and of *himself* by what he *feels*, in lowliness of heart he esteems others better than himself... This is the warfare. But it shall not always be so. Grace shall prevail. The evil nature is already enervated [lacking power], and ere long it shall die the death. Jesus will make us more than conquerors.

(*Cardiphonia,* 'Two Letters to Miss F...', Letter 2).

Suggested Scripture readings: Romans 6:17-23; Hebrews 12:14; 1 John 1:5 – 2:5

'*May the God of peace himself sanctify you entirely; and may your spirit and soul and body be preserved complete, without blame at the coming of our Lord Jesus Christ*' (1 Thess. 5:23).

Blemished biographies

In this creative letter, Newton warns his readers against various sins that are considered by some as too trivial to address. His warning takes the form of miniature biographies of imaginary Christians who have 'minor' blemishes that plague their otherwise admirable character. I must confess that as I read each of these clever portraits, it was tempting to assign the names of real people I know to these fictitious persons. But on further reflection, I admit that I see parts of myself in each of these regrettable characters.

AUSTERUS is a solid and exemplary Christian. He has a deep, extensive, and experimental knowledge of divine things. Inflexibly and invariably true to his principles, he stems [i.e. stands firm against], with a noble singularity, the torrent of the world, and can neither be bribed nor intimidated from the path of duty. He is a rough diamond of great intrinsic value, and would sparkle with a distinguished lustre if he were more polished; but, though the Word of God is his daily study ... there is one precept he seems to have overlooked; I mean that of the apostle: 'Be courteous.' Instead of that gentleness and condescension [i.e. graciousness] which will always be expected from a professed follower of the meek and lowly Jesus, there is a harshness in his manner which makes him more admired than beloved; and they who truly love him often feel more constraint than pleasure when in his company. His intimate friends are satisfied that he is no stranger to true humility of heart; but these are few; by others he is thought proud, dogmatic, and self-important; nor can this prejudice against him be easily removed until he can lay aside that cynical air which he has unhappily contracted.

HUMANUS is generous and benevolent. His feelings are lively, and his expressions of them strong. No one is more distant from sordid views, or less influenced by a selfish spirit. His heart burns with love to Jesus, and he is ready to receive with open arms all who love his Saviour. Yet, with an upright and friendly spirit, which entitles him to the love and esteem of all who know him, he has not everything we would wish in a friend. In some respects, though not in the most criminal sense, he bridleth not his tongue. Should you, without witness or writing, entrust him with untold gold, you would run no risk of loss; but if you entrust him with a secret, you thereby put it in the possession of the public. Not that he would wilfully betray you, but it is his infirmity: he knows not how to keep a secret; it escapes from him before he is aware. So likewise as to matters of fact: in things which are of great importance, and where he is sufficiently informed, no man has a stricter regard to truth; but in the smaller concerns of common life, whether it be from credulity, or from a strange and blameable inadvertence, he frequently grieves and surprises those who know his real character by saying *the thing that is not...* How lamentable are such blemishes in such a person! ...

CESSATOR is not chargeable with being buried in the cares and business of the present life to the neglect of the one thing needful; but he greatly neglects the duties of his station. Had he been sent into the world only to read, pray, hear sermons, and join in religious conversation, he might pass for an eminent Christian. But though it is to be hoped that his abounding in these exercises springs from a heart-attachment to divine things, his conduct evidences that his judgement is weak, and his views of his Christian calling are very narrow and defective. He does not consider that waiting upon God in the public and private ordinances is designed, not to excuse us from the discharge of the duties of civil life, but to instruct, strengthen, and qualify us for their performance. His affairs are in disorder, and his family and connections are likely to suffer by his indolence. He thanks God that he is not worldly-minded, but he is an idle and unfaithful member of society, and causes the way of truth to be evil spoken of. Of such, the apostle has determined that 'If any man will not work, neither should he eat.'

CURIOSUS is upright and unblameable in his general deportment, and no stranger to the experience of a true Christian. His conversation upon these subjects is often satisfactory and edifying. He would be a much more agreeable companion, were it not for an impertinent desire of knowing everybody's business, and the grounds of every hint that is occasionally dropped in discourse when he is present. This puts him upon asking a multiplicity of needless and improper questions, and obliges those who know him to be continually upon their guard, and to treat him with reserve... For this idle curiosity he is marked and avoided as a busybody, and they who have the best opinion of him cannot but wonder that a man who appears to have so many better things to employ his thoughts should find leisure to amuse himself with what does not at all concern him. Were it not for the rules of civility, he would be affronted every day; and if he would attend to the cold and evasive answers he receives to his enquiries, or even to the looks with which they are accompanied, he might learn that, though he means no harm, he appears to a great disadvantage, and that this prying disposition is very unpleasing.

QUERULUS wastes much of his precious time in declaiming against the management of public affairs; though he has neither access to the springs which move the wheels of government, nor influence to accelerate or retard their motions... This would be a weakness if we consider him only as a member of society, but if we consider him as a Christian, it is worse than weakness; it is a sinful conformity to the men of the world, who look no farther than to second causes, and forget that the Lord reigns... Our Lord's kingdom is not of this world; and most of his people may do their country much more essential service by pleading for it in prayer, than by finding fault with things which they have no power to alter.

(Forty-one Letters on Religious Subjects, Letter 35)

S uggested Scripture readings: Psalms 26:1-12; 139:23-24; Proverbs 17:3

> *'Who can discern his errors? Acquit me of hidden faults. Also keep back your servant from presumptuous sins'* (Ps. 19:12-13).

Satan's mirror

In the following excerpts, Newton points out that when sin is examined in the light of God's Word and the sufferings of Christ on the cross, it appears hideous, repulsive and an utterly insane choice. However, Satan often deceives by holding up his 'glass', which, like trick mirrors in an amusement park or at a carnival, distorts the perception of sin, making it appear attractive and reasonable.

Sin is the burden under which [a believer] groans; and he would account nothing short of a deliverance from it worthy of the name of salvation. A principal part of his evidence that he is a believer arises from that abhorrence of sin which he habitually feels. It is true, sin still dwelleth in him; but he loathes and resists it; upon this account he is in a state of continual warfare; if he was not so, he could not have the witness in himself that he is born of God. We may be afraid of the consequences of sin from other considerations, but it is only by looking to him who was pierced for our transgressions that we can learn to hate it.

(Forty-One Letters on Religious Subjects, Letter 8)

[In the words, 'He spared not his own Son'] we may see
the evil of sin. The bitter fruits are indeed visible every-
where. Sin is the cause of all the labour, sickness, pain, and
grief under which the whole creation groans. Sin often
makes man a terror and a burden, both to himself and those
about him... For this [i.e. on account of sin], a shower of
brimstone fell upon a whole country; for this, an overwhelming deluge destroyed a whole world; for this, princi-
palities and powers were cast from heaven, and are reserved under 'chains of darkness' (2 Peter 2) to a more
dreadful doom. But none of these things, nor all of them
together, afford such a conviction of the heinous nature and
destructive effects of sin as we may gather from these
words: 'He spared not his own Son.'

(*Six Discourses as Intended for the Pulpit*, Sermon 4)

That sin is a great evil is evident by its effects. It deprived Adam of the life and presence of God, and brought
death and all natural evil into the world. It caused the destruction of the old world by water. It is the source of all the
misery with which the earth is now filled; it will kindle the
last great conflagration [i.e. the fire of God's judgement];
yea, it has already kindled that fire which shall never be
quenched. But in no view does the sinfulness of sin appear
so striking as in this wonderful effect — the suffering and
death of Messiah: that notwithstanding the dignity of his
person, and the perfection of his obedience to the law, and
that though he prayed in his agonies that if it were possible
the cup might pass from him [Luke 22:42], yet, if sinners
were to be saved, it was indispensably necessary that he
should drink it. This shows the evil of sin in the strongest
light; and in this light it is viewed by all who derive life
from his death, and healing from his wounds.

(*Fifty sermons preached on Handel's 'The Messiah'*, Sermon 20)

Sin's deceit

S in, when viewed by Scripture light,
 Is a horrid, hateful sight;
But when seen in Satan's glass,
Then it wears a pleasing face.

When the gospel trumpet sounds,
When I think how grace abounds,
When I feel sweet peace within,
Then I'd rather die than sin.

When the cross I view by faith,
Sin is madness, poison, death;
Tempt me not, 'tis all in vain;
Sure I ne'er can yield again.

Satan, for a while debarred,
When he finds me off my guard,
Puts his glass before my eyes;
Quickly other thoughts arise.

What before excited fears
Rather pleasing now appears;
If a sin, it seems so small,
Or, perhaps, no sin at all.

Often thus, through sin's deceit,
Grief, and shame, and loss I meet;
Like a fish, my soul mistook,
Saw the bait, but not the hook.

O my Lord, what shall I say?
How can I presume to pray?
Not a word have I to plead;
Sins like mine are black indeed!

Made, by past experience, wise,
Let me learn thy Word to prize;
Taught by what I've felt before,
Let me Satan's glass abhor.

(*Olney Hymns*, Book 3, Hymn 76)

Suggested Scripture readings: Romans 1:18-32; Ephesians 2:1-3; James 1:13-18

'You are those who justify yourselves in the sight of men, but God knows your hearts; for that which is highly esteemed among men is detestable in the sight of God' (Luke 16:15).

Holy ambition

In this letter, Newton reminds us of three aspects of what should be the holy ambition of every believer: first, a satisfaction in God that makes us indifferent to all worldly delights; secondly, a joyful submission to God's will that is grounded in the goodness and sovereignty of God; and, thirdly, a preoccupation with the glory of God that replaces our preoccupation with self. With endearing characteristic humility, Newton follows his profound admonishment with the honest confession of his own failure to live up to what he himself has just written.

Weak, unskilled, and unfaithful as I am in practice, the Lord has been pleased to give me some idea of what a Christian ought to be, and of what is actually attainable in this present life, by those whom he enables earnestly to aspire towards the prize of their high calling... Permit me to mention two or three particulars, in which those who have a holy ambition of aspiring to them shall not be altogether disappointed...

1. *A delight in the Lord's all-sufficiency*, to be satisfied in him as our present and eternal portion... [This is the result of] a deeply rooted and abiding principle, the habitual exercise of which is to be estimated by the comparative indifference with which other things are regarded. The soul thus principled is not at leisure to take or seek satisfaction in anything but what has a known subserviency to this leading taste. Either the Lord is present, and then he is to be rejoiced in; or else he is absent, and then he is to be sought and waited for. They are to be pitied who, if they are at some times happy in the Lord, can at other times be happy without him, and rejoice in broken cisterns, when their spirits are at a distance from the fountain of living waters... What a privilege is this, to possess God in all things while we have them, and all things in God when they are taken from us!

2. *An acquiescence in* [i.e. submission to] *the Lord's will* founded in a persuasion of his wisdom, holiness, sovereignty, and goodness... Our own limited views, and short-sighted purposes and desires may be, and will be, often overruled; but then our main and leading desire, that the will of the Lord may be done, must be accomplished. How highly does it become us, both as creatures and as sinners, to submit to the appointments of our Maker! And how necessary is it to our peace! This great attainment is too often unthought of, and overlooked; we are prone to fix our attention upon the second causes and immediate instruments of events, forgetting that whatever befalls us is according to his purpose, and therefore must be right and seasonable in itself, and shall in the issue be productive of good [i.e. will produce a good outcome]. From hence arise impatience, resentment, and secret repinings [i.e. murmurings], which are not only sinful, but tormenting: whereas, if all things are in his hand; if the very hairs of our head are numbered; if every event, great and small, is under the

direction of his providence and purpose; and if he has a wise, holy, and gracious end in view, to which everything that happens is subordinate and subservient — then we have nothing to do, but with patience and humility to follow as he leads, and cheerfully to expect a happy issue [i.e. outcome]. The path of present duty is marked out, and the concerns of the next and every succeeding hour are in his hands. How happy are they who can resign all to him, see his hands in every dispensation [i.e. circumstance], and believe that he chooses better for them than they possibly could for themselves!

3. *A single eye to his glory*, as the ultimate scope of all our undertakings. The Lord can design nothing short of his own glory, nor should we. The constraining love of Christ has a direct and marvellous tendency, in proportion to the measure of faith, to mortify the corrupt principle, Self, which for a season is the grand spring of our conduct, and by which we are too much biased after we know the Lord. But as grace prevails, self is renounced. We feel that we are not our own, that we are bought with a price; and that it is our duty, our honour, and our happiness to be the servants of God and of the Lord Jesus Christ. To devote soul and body, every talent, power, and faculty to the service of his cause and will; to let our light shine (in our several situations) to the praise of his grace; to place our highest joy in the contemplation of his adorable perfections; to rejoice even in tribulations and distresses, in reproaches and infirmities, if thereby the power of Christ may rest upon us, and be magnified in us; to be content, yea glad, to be nothing, that he may be all in all; to obey *him*, in opposition to the threats or solicitations of men; to trust *him*, though all outward appearances seem against us; to rejoice in *him*, though we should (as will sooner or later be the case) have nothing else to rejoice in; to live above the world, and to have our conversation [i.e. way of life] in heaven [Philippians 3:20]; to be

like the angels, finding our own pleasure in performing his — this … is the prize, the mark of our high calling, to which we are encouraged with a holy ambition continually to aspire. It is true, we shall still fall short; we shall find that, when we would do good, evil will be present with us. But the attempt is glorious, and shall not wholly be in vain. He that gives us thus *to will* will enable us to perform with growing success, and teach us to profit even by our mistakes and imperfections.

I hope I *may* say that I *desire* to be thus entirely given up to the Lord; I am sure I *must* say that what I have written is far from being my actual experience. Alas! I might be condemned out of my own mouth, were the Lord strict to mark what is amiss. But — oh, the comfort! — we are not under law, but under grace… *There* is the unshaken ground of hope — a reconciled Father, a prevailing Advocate, a powerful Shepherd, a compassionate Friend, a Saviour who is able and willing to save to the uttermost. He knows our frame; he remembers that we are but dust; and has opened for us a new and blood-besprinkled way of access to the throne of grace, that we may obtain mercy, and find grace to help in every time of need.

(*Cardiphonia*, 'Twenty-Six Letters to a Nobleman', Letter 7).

*S*uggested Scripture reading: Psalm 73

'Whom have I in heaven but you? And besides you, I desire nothing on earth' (Ps. 73:25).

On modesty

As I worked on the initial stages of this book, I was on a period of sabbatical leave from ministering at my own dear church, and as a result my family and I had the opportunity to worship in other churches for a few months. During our visits, I must confess that, on one particular Sunday, I was shocked and appalled to see two young teenage girls saunter casually across the church wearing (barely!) exceedingly short denim cut-off shorts and flip-flops. Such an outfit at the beach would have offended me, but at a service appointed for the worship of the living God, I was unspeakably grieved! Perhaps these foolish young ladies were not Christians and had been brought by a friend to hear the gospel preached. I hope so, but my experience in the ministry over the last twenty years makes me aware that, unfortunately, those girls could easily have been the pastor's children! I could not help but ask, as I have at many points over the years, 'Lord, what is wrong with the church today? What is wrong with those young ladies' fathers, that they would allow them to walk out of the door like that? Where was the guidance of those girls' mothers as they dressed for worship that morning?'

In the following letter published in a periodical, Newton asks similar questions and expresses his own concern about women dressing in a way that is appropriate to their profession of faith. Notice how his needed pastoral instruction avoids legalism by not only addressing external standards of attire but also, and more importantly, exposing the sinful motives in the heart of those whose dress is immodest. If Newton was alarmed by what he observed among those who filled the pews of the churches of eighteenth-century England, what would he have said of the situation today? The issues he addresses sound frighteningly contemporary. This same note of warning needs to be sounded again in our day, by both parents and pastors, with similar directness, warmth and courage.

> I doubt not but many parents who desire to see their children brought up in the nurture and admonition of the Lord give them many excellent lessons in the nursery ... but ... for want of due reflection, or resolution, or both, they either encourage, or at least permit, them, to form habits [i.e.

in dress], which have a direct tendency to counteract all the benefits which might otherwise be hoped for from the instruction of their early years...

A nice [i.e. a particular] attention to dress will cost you much of what is more valuable than money — your precious time. It will too much occupy your thoughts... And it certainly administers [i.e. provides] fuel to that latent fire of pride and vanity which is inseparable from our fallen nature, and is easily blown up into a blaze... If a woman, when going to public worship, looks in the glass, and contemplates, with a secret self-complacence [i.e. satisfaction], the figure which it reflects to her view, I am afraid she is not in the frame of spirit most suitable for one who is about to cry for mercy as a miserable sinner...

I am not so much hurt by observing the materials, as by the manner of female dress; by what we call the fashion, and the eagerness with which every changing fashion, however improper, is adopted, by persons whose religious profession might lead us to hope they had no leisure to attend to such trifles. If some allowance is to be made for youth on this head [i.e. in this matter], it is painful to see mothers, and possibly sometimes grandmothers, who seem, by the gaudiness and levity of their attire, very unwilling to be sensible [i.e. aware] that they are growing older...

Why should a godly woman, or one who wishes to be thought so, make herself ridiculous [by her immodest dress], or hazard a suspicion of her character, to please and imitate an ungodly world ...?

The worst of all the fashions are those which are evidently calculated to allure the eyes, and to draw the attention of [the male] sex. Is it not strange that modest and even pious women should be seduced into a compliance even with these [alluring fashion trends]? Yet I have sometimes been in company with ladies of whose modesty I have no doubt, and of whose piety I entertained a good hope, when I have been embarrassed, and at a loss which way to look. They are indeed noticed by the men, but not to their honour nor advantage. The manner of their dress gives encouragement to vile and insidious men, and exposes them to dangerous temptations. This inconsiderate levity has often proved the first step into the road that leads to misery and ruin. They are pleased with the flattery of the worthless, and go on without thought, 'as a bird hastens to the snare, and knoweth not that it is for its life' [Proverbs 7:23]. But honest and sensible men regard their exterior [i.e. their outward appearance] as a warning signal, not to choose a companion for life from among persons of this light and volatile turn of mind.

An attention to ornament and dress is peculiarly unseasonable at present. The dark aspect of the times requires a spirit of humiliation and abasement. The judgements of God are abroad; his hand is lifted up. We know not what is before us, but we have reason to fear awful tokens of his displeasure for our national sins. Perhaps the day is coming when the words of the prophet, 'Tremble, ye women that are at ease, be afflicted, ye careless ones' [Isaiah 32:11], may be no less applicable to us than they were to the Israelites of old. I earnestly request my fair readers carefully to peruse the latter part of the third chapter of the prophecy of Isaiah, from the sixteenth verse to the end.

(*The Works of John Newton,* vol. 6, 'Miscellaneous papers extracted from periodical publications')

S uggested Scripture reading: Isaiah 3:16-26; 1 Peter 3:3-4; 1 Timothy 2:9-10

> '*Likewise, I want women to adorn themselves with proper clothing, modestly and discreetly ... as is proper for women making a claim to godliness*' (I Tim. 2:9-10).

A pervasive faith

In this letter Newton affirms the truth that all those who have been *declared* righteous by God (justified) will also progressively begin to *be* righteous (sanctified) in their lifestyle. He strings together a catalogue of areas of everyday life that are affected by a real and living faith. Since we are all prone to compartmentalize our faith, the truths in this letter admonish us concerning the demands of faith in every aspect of our lives.

The use and importance of faith, as it respects a sinner's justification before God, has been largely insisted on; but it is likewise of great use and importance in the daily concerns of life. It gives evidence and subsistence to things not seen, and realizes the great truths of the gospel, so as that they become abiding and living principles of support and direction while we are passing through this wilderness...

The faith which justifies the soul does likewise receive from Jesus grace for grace, whereby the heart is purified, and the conversation [i.e. lifestyle] regulated as becomes the gospel of Christ...

Whosoever is possessed of true faith will not confine his enquiries to the single point of his acceptance before God, or be satisfied with the distant hope of heaven hereafter. He will be likewise solicitous how he may glorify God in the world, and enjoy such foretastes of heaven as are attainable while he is yet upon earth...

By faith he is enabled to use prosperity with moderation; and knows and feels that what the world calls good is of small value, unless it is accompanied with the presence and blessings of him whom his soul loveth. And his faith upholds him under all trials, by assuring him that every dispensation [i.e. circumstance] is under the direction of his Lord; that chastisements are a token of his love; that the season, measure, and continuance of his sufferings are appointed by infinite wisdom, and designed to work for his everlasting good; and that grace and strength shall be afforded him. according to his day, Thus, his heart being fixed, trusting in the Lord, to whom he has committed all his concerns, and knowing that his best interests are safe, he is not greatly afraid of evil tidings, but enjoys a stable peace in the midst of a changing world...

By the same principle of faith, a believer's conduct is regulated towards his fellow-creatures; and in the discharge of the several duties and relations of life, his great aim is to please God, and to let his light shine in the world... From the same views by faith he derives a benevolent spirit, and, according to his sphere and ability, he endeavours to promote the welfare of all around him. The law of love being thus written in his heart, and his soul set at liberty from the low and narrow dictates of a selfish spirit, his language will be truth, and his dealings equity. His promise may be depended on, without the interposition of oath, bond, or witness; and the feelings of his own heart, under the direction of an enlightened conscience, and the precepts of Scripture, prompt him 'to do unto others as he would desire they, in the like circumstances, should do unto him'. If he is a master, he is gentle and compassionate; if a servant, he is faithful and obedient; for in either relation he acts by faith, under the eye of his Master in heaven. If he is a trader, he neither dares nor wishes to take advantage either of the ignorance or the necessities of those with whom he deals. And the same principle of love influences his whole conversation [i.e. lifestyle]. A sense of his own infirmities makes him candid to those of others: he will not readily believe reports to their prejudice, without sufficient proof; and even then, he will not repeat them, unless he is lawfully called to it. He believes that the precept, 'Speak evil of no man,' is founded upon the same authority with those which forbid committing adultery or murder; and therefore he 'keeps his tongue as with a bridle'.

Lastly, faith is of daily use as a preservative from a compliance with the corrupt customs and maxims of the world. The believer, though *in* the world, is not *of* it: by faith he triumphs over its smiles and enticements; he sees that all that is in the world, suited to gratify the desires of the flesh or the eye, is not only to be avoided as sinful, but as incompatible with his best pleasures. He will mix with the world so far as is necessary, in the discharge of the duties of that station of life in which the providence of God has placed him, but no farther. His leisure and inclinations are engaged in a different pursuit. They who fear the Lord are his chosen companions; and the blessings he derives from the Word, and throne, and ordinances of grace make him look upon the poor pleasures and amusements of those who live without God in the world with a mixture of disdain and pity. And by faith he is proof against its frowns. He will obey God rather than man; he will 'have no fellowship with the unfruitful works of darkness, but will rather reprove them'. And if, upon this account, he should be despised and injuriously treated, whatever loss he suffers in such a cause, he accounts his gain, and esteems such disgrace [to be] his glory.

I am not aiming to draw a perfect character, but to show the proper effects of that faith which justifies, which purifies the heart, worketh by love, and overcomes the world. A habitual endeavour to possess such a frame of spirit, and thus to adorn the gospel of Christ, and that with growing success, is what I am persuaded you are not a stranger to; and I am afraid that they who can content themselves with aiming at anything short of this in their profession are too much strangers to themselves, and to the nature of that liberty wherewith Jesus has promised to make his people free.

(*Forty-one Letters on Religious Subjects,* Letter 6)

Suggested Scripture readings: Ephesians 4:1-3,17-32

> *'Walk in a manner worthy of the calling with which you have been called'* (Eph. 4:1).

Counselling yourself

When most people think of the book of Psalms, they think of words of exuberant praise and enthusiastic thanksgiving. But it is important to keep in mind that approximately half of the 150 psalms are lament psalms — that is, sad songs that plead with God for help. Psalm 42 and 43, which were probably originally one song, are examples of many lament psalms in which we 'overhear' the psalmist as he counsels his own despairing soul — alternately questioning and admonishing his dark thoughts. Rather than listening to our feelings, we would do well to follow the example of these two psalms and learn to practise the art of telling ourselves what we know to be objectively true from the Word of God, no matter what our feelings are saying! The two hymns that follow are based on these two lament psalms.

Why art thou cast down?

*B*e still, my heart! These anxious cares
To thee are burdens, thorns, and snares,
They cast dishonour on thy Lord,
And contradict his gracious Word!

Brought safely by his hand thus far,
Why wilt thou now give place to fear?
How canst thou want if he provide,
Or lose thy way with such a guide?

When first before his mercy seat,
Thou didst to him thy all commit;
He gave thee warrant, from that hour,
To trust his wisdom, love, and power.

Did ever trouble yet befall,
And he refuse to hear thy call?
And has he not his promise past,
That thou shalt overcome at last?

Like David, thou mayst comfort draw,
Saved from the bear's and lion's paw;
Goliath's rage I may defy,
For God, my Saviour, still is nigh.

He who has helped me hitherto
Will help me all my journey through;
And give me daily cause to raise
New Ebenezers to his praise.

Though rough and thorny be the road,
It leads thee home, apace, to God;
Then count thy present trials small,
For heaven will make amends for all.

(*Olney Hymns*, Book 3, Hymn 40)

The prisoner

*W*hen the poor prisoner through a grate [i.e. grating]
Sees others walk at large,
How does he mourn his lonely state
And long for a discharge?

Thus I, confined in unbelief,
My loss of freedom mourn;

And spend my hours in fruitless grief,
Until my Lord return.

The beam of day, which pierces through
The gloom in which I dwell,
Only discloses to my view
The horrors of my cell.

Ah! How my pensive spirit faints,
To think of former days,
When I could triumph with the saints,
And join their songs of praise!

But now my joys are all cut off;
In prison I am cast;
And Satan, with a cruel scoff,
Says, 'Where's your God at last?'

Dear Saviour, for thy mercies' sake,
My strong, my only plea,
These gates and bars in pieces break,
And set the prisoner free!

Surely my soul shall sing to thee,
For liberty restored;
And all thy saints admire to see
The mercies of the Lord.

(*Olney Hymns*, Book 3, Hymn 34)

The letter from which the following excerpts are taken also provides wonderful advice on how the unchanging truth of God's Word can console and confront our vacillating feelings.

We all need, and at the seasons the Lord sees best we all receive, chastisement…

We are like trees, which, though alive, cannot put forth
their leaves and fruit without the influence of the sun. They
are alive in winter as well as in summer; but how different
is their appearance in these different seasons! Were we always alike, could we always believe, love, and rejoice, we
should think the power inherent, and our own; but it is
more for the Lord's glory, and more suited to form us to a
temper becoming [i.e. befitting] the gospel, that we should
be made deeply sensible of our own inability and dependence, than that we should always be in a lively frame [i.e. in
a cheerful frame of mind]. I am persuaded a broken and
contrite spirit, a conviction of our vileness and nothingness,
connected with a cordial acceptance of Jesus as revealed in
the gospel, is the highest attainment we can reach in this
life. Sensible [i.e. felt] comforts are desirable and we must be
sadly declined when they do not appear to us; but I believe
there may be a real exercise of faith and growth in grace
when our sensible feelings are faint and low. A soul may be
in as thriving a state when thirsting, seeking, and mourning
after the Lord as when actually rejoicing in him; as much in
earnest when fighting in the valley as when singing upon
the mount; nay, dark seasons afford the surest and strongest
manifestations of the power of faith. To hold fast the word
of promise, to maintain a hatred of sin, to go on steadfastly
in the path of duty, in defiance both of the frowns and the
smiles of the world, when we have but little comfort, is a
more certain evidence of grace than a thousand things
which we may do or forbear when our spirits are warm and
lively. I have seen many who have been, upon the whole,
but uneven walkers [inconsistent in their walk with the
Lord], though at times they have seemed to enjoy, at least
have talked of, great comforts. I have seen others, for the
most part, complain of much darkness and coldness, who
have been remarkably humble, tender, and exemplary in

their spirit and conduct. Surely, were I to choose my lot, it
should be with the latter.

(*Cardiphonia*, 'Seven Letters to the Rev. Mr P...,' Letter 7)

*S*uggested Scripture readings: Psalm 42:1 – 43:5

'*Why are you in despair, O my soul? And why have you become
disturbed within me?*' (Ps. 42:5).

Real humility

In these letters that follow, Newton reminds believers of the utter
necessity of humility in a Christian's life. But he also provides them
with the gentle warning that growing in humility is directly tied to
growing in the painful knowledge of the enormous sinfulness of their
own hearts.

The Christian's temper [i.e. disposition] God-ward is
evidenced by *humility*. He has received from Gethsemane
and Golgotha such a sense of the evil of sin, and of the holiness of God, combined with his matchless love for sinners,
as has deeply penetrated his heart: he has an affecting remembrance of the state of rebellion and enmity in which he
once lived against this holy and good God; and he has a
quick perception of the defilements and defects which still
debase his best services. His mouth is therefore stopped as
to boasting; he is vile in his own eyes, and is filled with
wonder that the Lord should visit such a sinner with such
salvation. He sees so vast a disproportion between the obligations he is under to grace and the returns he makes that
he is disposed, yea constrained, to adopt the apostle's

words, without affectation, and to account himself less than
the least of all the saints; and, knowing his own *heart* while
he sees only the *outside* of others, he is not easily persuaded
[that] there can be a believer upon earth so faint, so unfruitful, so unworthy as himself. Yet, though abased, he is not
discouraged, for he enjoys peace.

(*Cardiphonia*, 'Twenty-Six Letters to a Nobleman', Letter 24)

To be humble, and, like a little child, afraid of taking a
step alone, and so conscious of snares and dangers around
us as to cry to him continually to hold us up that we may be
safe, is the sure, the infallible, the only secret of walking
closely with him.

But how shall we attain this humble fame of spirit? It
must be, as I said, from a real and sensible [i.e. conscious]
conviction of our weakness and vileness, which we cannot
learn (at least I have not been able to learn it) merely from
books or preachers. The providence of God concurs with his
Holy Spirit in his merciful design of making us acquainted
with ourselves.

(*Cardiphonia*, 'Two Letters to Miss F...,' Letter 1)

Indeed, we cannot value [humility] too highly; for we
can be neither comfortable, safe, nor habitually useful,
without it. The root of pride lies deep in our fallen nature,
and, where the Lord has given natural and acquired abilities, it would grow apace, if he did not mercifully watch
over us, and suit his dispensations [i.e. dealings with us] to
keep it down.

(*Cardiphonia*, 'Five Letters to Mr C...', Letter 1)

If the Lord is pleased to bless you, he will undoubtedly
make you humble; for you cannot be either happy or safe, or
have any probable hope of abiding usefulness, without it. I
do not know that I have had anything so much at heart in

my connections with you, as to impress you with a sense of
the necessity and advantages of an humble frame of spirit:
Oh, to be little in our own eyes! This is the groundwork of
every grace; this leads to a continual dependence upon the
Lord Jesus; this is the spirit that he has promised to bless …
for he that abaseth [i.e. humbles] himself is sure to be hon-
oured… For are we not sinners? Were we not rebels and
enemies before we knew the gospel? And have we not been
unfaithful, backsliding, and unprofitable ever since? Are we
not redeemed by the blood of Jesus? And can we stand a
single moment except he upholds us? Have we anything
that we have not received: or have we received anything that
we have not abused? Why then is dust and ashes proud?

(*Cardiphonia*, Five Letters to Mr …, Letter 2)

The hymn below describes what Newton considered to be the
more than ample reasons for his own personal humility. If this great
man of God considered himself a vile and unfit dwelling for God,
still swarming with sins, how much more humbled should you and I
be!

Behold, I am vile!

O Lord, how vile am I,
   Unholy, and unclean!
How can I dare to venture nigh
With such a load of sin?

Is this polluted heart
A dwelling fit for thee?
Swarming, alas! in every part,
What evils do I see!

If I attempt to pray,
And lisp thy holy name,

My thoughts are hurried soon away;
I know not where I am.

If in thy Word I look,
Such darkness fills my mind,
I only read a sealed book,
But no relief can find.

Thy gospel oft I hear,
But hear it still in vain;
Without desire, or love, or fear,
I like a stone remain.

Myself can hardly bear
This wretched heart of mine;
How hateful then must it appear
To those pure eyes of thine!

And must I then indeed
Sink in despair and die?
Fain would I hope that thou didst bleed
For such a wretch as I.

That blood which thou hast spilt,
That grace which is thine own,
Can cleanse the vilest sinner's guilt,
And soften hearts of stone.

Low at thy feet I bow;
Oh, pity and forgive!
Here will I lie and wait, till thou
Shalt bid me rise and live.

(Olney Hymns, Book 3, Hymn 7)

*S*uggested **Scripture readings:** Proverbs 11:2; 15:33; Isaiah 57:15; James 4:10; 1 Peter 5:5-11

'Clothe yourselves with humility toward one another, for God is opposed to the proud but gives grace to the humble' (1 Peter 5:5).

God's purposes in trials

These inward trials

Within the *Olney Hymnal* there is a group of hymns 'On the Rise, Progress, Changes, and Comforts of the Spiritual Life'. In one of the hymns from this section, entitled 'Prayers Answered by Crosses', Newton candidly records how he learnt by personal experience that there are no pain-free shortcuts on the path to spiritual growth. He confesses that he had naively believed that 'in some favoured hour *all at once*' God would answer his request to subdue completely the sin still remaining in his life.

Newton admits that he was surprised, even dismayed, when God did not provide the instantaneous deliverance for which he had hoped, but chose instead to reveal to him even more sin — sins of which he had been unaware, and which he calls the 'hidden evils' of his heart. God's ultimate purpose in revealing such sin, however, was not merely to humble him, but to show him the utter vanity of seeking joy in anything in this world.

Prayers answered by crosses

1 asked the Lord that I might grow
In faith, and love, and every grace;
Might more of his salvation know,
And seek, more earnestly, his face.

'Twas he who taught me thus to pray,
And he, I trust, has answered prayer;
But it has been in such a way
As almost drove me to despair.

I hoped that in some favoured hour,
At once he'd answer my request;
And by his love's constraining power,
Subdue my sins, and give me rest.

Instead of this, he made me feel
The hidden evils of my heart;
And let the angry powers of hell
Assault my soul in every part.

Yea, more, with his own hand he seemed
Intent to aggravate my woe,
Crossed all the fair designs I schemed,
Blasted my gourds [i.e. took away my comforts], [5] and laid
    me low.

'Lord, why is this?' I trembling cried,
'Wilt thou pursue thy worm to death?'
' 'Tis in this way', the Lord replied,
'I answer prayer for grace and faith.

'These inward trials I employ,
From self, and pride, to set thee free;
And break thy schemes for earthly joy,
That thou mayst find thy all in me.'
                        (*Olney Hymns*, Book 3, Hymn 36)

This text is especially dear to me for several reasons. First, it parallels my own past spiritual expectations and disappointments. In the early days of my Christian life, I too believed that there were certain experiences that would produce a sudden and dramatic leap forward in my spiritual maturity, 'all at once'. In time, I became disillusioned by my extremely slow and undramatic progress towards Christlikeness. What comfort came to me later when I learned from Scripture that slow and steady progress towards holiness and an ever-increasing awareness of my own indwelling sin (which made my progress seem even slower) were actually quite normal!

Suggested **Scripture readings:** Psalm 119:67,71,75; 2 Corinthians 4:16-18; 1 Peter 4:12-13; 5:10

> *'After you have suffered for a little while, the God of all grace, who called you to his eternal glory in Christ, will himself perfect, confirm, strengthen and establish you. To him be dominion for ever and ever. Amen'* (1 Peter 5:10).

Good fruit from a bitter root

Below is a portion of a letter which Newton wrote as a follow-up to an earlier solemn letter to Lord Dartmouth on 'the mournful subject of the depravity of the heart'. In it he encourages the nobleman to remain focused on the 'gracious purposes of God' as he reveals our sin to us in its unvarnished ugliness.

The gracious purposes to which the Lord makes the sense and feeling of our depravity subservient are manifold. Hereby his own power, wisdom, faithfulness, and love are more signally displayed — his power, in maintaining his own work in the midst of so much opposition, like a spark burning in the water, or a bush unconsumed in the flames; his wisdom, in defeating and controlling all the devices which Satan, from his knowledge of the evil of our nature, is encouraged to practise against us... The unchangeableness of the Lord's love and the riches of his mercy are likewise more illustrated by the multiplied pardons he bestows upon his people than if they needed no forgiveness at all.

Hereby the Lord Jesus Christ is more endeared to the soul; all boasting is effectually excluded, and the glory of a full and free salvation is ascribed to him alone. If a mariner is surprised by a storm, and after one night spent in jeopardy is presently brought safe into port, though he may rejoice in his deliverance, it will not affect him so sensibly [i.e. it will not make such a profound impression on him] as if, after being tempest-tossed for a long season, and experiencing a great number and variety of hair-breadth escapes, he at last gains the desired haven. The righteous are said to be scarcely saved, not with respect to the certainty of the event, for the purpose of God in their favour cannot be disappointed, but in respect of their own apprehensions, and the great difficulties they are brought through. But when, after a long experience of their own deceitful hearts, after repeated proofs of their weakness, wilfulness, ingratitude, and insensibility, [believers] find that none of these things can separate them from the love of God in Christ, Jesus becomes more and more precious to their souls. They love much, because much has been forgiven them. They dare not, they will not ascribe anything to themselves, but are glad to acknowledge that they must have perished (if possible) a thousand times over, if Jesus had not been their Saviour, their Shepherd, and their shield. When they were wandering, he brought them back, when fallen he raised them, when wounded he healed them, when fainting he revived them. By him, out of weakness they have been made strong; he has taught their hands to war, and covered their heads in the day of battle. In a word, some of the clearest proofs they have had of his excellence have been occasioned by the mortifying proofs they have had of their own vileness. They would not have known so much of him, if they had not known so much of themselves.

Further, a spirit of humiliation ... is greatly promoted by our feeling, as well as reading, that when we would do good, evil is present with us. A broken and contrite spirit is pleasing to the Lord, who has promised to dwell with those who have it; and experience shows that the exercise of all our graces is in proportion to the humbling sense we have of the depravity of our nature. But that we are so totally depraved is a truth which no one ever truly learned by being only told it. Indeed, if we could receive, and habitually maintain a right judgement of ourselves, by what is plainly declared in Scripture, it would probably save us many a mournful hour; but experience is the Lord's school, and they who are taught by him usually learn that they have no wisdom by the mistakes they make, and that they have no strength by the slips and falls they meet with. Every day draws forth some new corruption which before was little observed, or at least discovers it in a stronger light than before. Thus by degrees they are weaned from leaning to any supposed wisdom, power, or goodness in themselves; they feel the truth of our Lord's words, 'Without me ye can do nothing', and the necessity of crying with David, 'Oh, lead me and guide me for thy name's sake...' The knowledge of [the Lord's] full and free forgiveness of thy innumerable backslidings and transgressions shall make thee ashamed, and silence the unruly workings of thine heart; thou shalt open thy mouth in praise; but thou shalt no more boast in thyself, or censure others, or repine at [God's] dispensations [i.e. acts of providence]. In these respects we are exceedingly prone to speak unadvisedly with our lips; but a sense of great unworthiness and much forgiveness checks these evils. Whoever is truly humbled will not be easily angry, will not be positive [i.e. self-assertive] and rash, will be compassionate and tender to the infirmities of his fellow-

sinners, knowing that, if there be a difference, it is grace that
has made it, and that he has the seeds of every evil in his
own heart; and, under all trials and afflictions, he will look
to the hand of the Lord, and lay his mouth in the dust, ac-
knowledging that he suffers much less than his iniquities
have deserved. These are some of the advantages and good
fruits which the Lord enables us to obtain from that bitter
root, indwelling sin.

(*Cardiphonia*, 'Twenty-Six Letters to a Nobleman', Letter 6)

The contrite heart
Isaiah 57:15

*T*he Lord will happiness divine
    On contrite hearts bestow;
Then tell me, gracious God, is mine
A contrite heart, or no?

I hear, but seem to hear in vain,
Insensible as steel;
If ought is felt, 'tis only pain,
To find I cannot feel.

I sometimes think myself inclined
To love thee, if I could;
But often feel another mind,
Averse to all that's good.

My best desires are faint and few;
I fain would strive for more,
But when I cry, 'My strength renew,'
Seem weaker than before.

Thy saints are comforted, I know,
And love thy house of prayer;

I therefore go where others go,
But find no comfort there.

Oh, make this heart rejoice, or ache!
Decide this doubt for me;
And if it be not broken, break,
And heal it, if it be.

(*Olney Hymns*, Book I, Hymn 64)

S uggested Scripture readings: Luke 7:36-50; James 1:1-12

> *'Search me, O God, and know my heart;*
> *Try me and know my ... thoughts;*
> *And see if there be any hurtful way in me,*
> *And lead me in the everlasting way'*
> (Ps. 139:23-24).

Tried like Abraham

Ten years after the death of his cherished wife of over forty years, Newton suffered another great trial. Betsy Catlett, his niece by marriage, whom he had raised as an adopted daughter since she was orphaned at the age of five, was taken ill with a 'nervous disorder' and institutionalized for twelve months. Newton's fatherly affection for her is captured in a letter he wrote to her as a child: 'One thing I can assure you, I mean that I am your very affectionate friend, and feel for you as if I was really and truly your father.' Imagine the agony of heart endured by the seventy-seven-year-old widower with failing health and eyesight, who needed help to walk once a day to Bedlam, the asylum to which she had been admitted. There he would stand outside to wave to the one whose sweet companionship had been such a comfort for twenty-seven years. He

The hospital of St Mary of Bethlehem, usually known as Bedlam, from a drawing dated 1784

would wait there until he was told that she had seen him and waved her handkerchief in return.

William Bull, a close friend of Newton, remarked that, during Betsy's illness Newton was 'almost overwhelmed with this most awful affliction. I never saw a man so cut up. He is almost broken-hearted.' The note reproduced below records Newton's prayer for sustaining grace during this time.

Happily, Betsy made a full recovery and when she later married, she and her husband made their home with Newton. Betsy was able to care for her adoptive father during his last years of illness until his death four years later.

If you were going through a time of suffering and your prayers were to be written down, would they at all resemble the one below? If not, then take note of Newton's prayer and follow his exemplary response to suffering and loss. His prayer contains a strong affirmation of God's goodness in the midst of heartache, a mature desire for God's glory, rather than his own comfort, a selfless sensitivity to the needs of others and, finally, a humble submission to God's will.

August 1st, 1801. I now enter my seventy-seventh year. I have been exercised this year with a trying and unexpected change; but it is by thy appointment, my gracious Lord, and thou art unchangeably wise, good and merciful. Thou gavest me my dear adopted child. Thou didst own my endeavours to bring her up for thee. I have no doubt that thou hast called her by thy grace. I thank thee for the many years' comfort I have had in her; and for the attention and affection she has always shown me, exceeding that of most daughters to their own parents.

Thou hast now tried me, as thou didst Abraham, in my old age; when my eyes are failing, and my strength declines. Thou hast called for my Isaac, who had so long been my chief stay and staff; but it was thy blessing that made her so. A nervous disorder has seized her, and I desire to leave her under thy care; and chiefly pray for myself, that I may be enabled to wait thy time and will, without betraying any signs of impatience or despondency unbecoming my profession and character. Hitherto thou hast helped me, and to thee I look for help in future.

Let all issue in thy glory, that my friends and hearers may be encouraged by seeing how I am supported: let thy strength be manifested in my weakness, and thy grace be sufficient for me, and let all finally work together for our good. Amen!

I am to say from my heart, 'Not my will but thine be done.' But though thou hast in a measure made my spirit willing, thou knowest, and I feel, that the flesh is weak. Lord, I believe; help thou my unbelief. Lord, I submit; subdue every rebellious thought that dares arise against thy will. Spare my eyes, if it please thee; but, above all, strengthen my faith and love.

(A hand-written note on some blank leaves in an edition of Newton's *Letters to a Wife*)[6]

*S*uggested **Scripture readings:** Psalm 34:18-22; Isaiah
42:1-3; 43:1-2; 2 Corinthians 12:7-10

> 'The LORD is near to the broken-hearted
> And saves those who are crushed in spirit.
> Many are the afflictions of the righteous,
> But the LORD delivers him out of them all'
> (Ps. 34:18-19).

3.

SPIRITUAL DISCIPLINES

Let us love, and sing, and wonder,
Let us praise the Saviour's name!
He has hushed the law's loud thunder,
He has quenched Mount Sinai's flame:
He has washed us with his blood,
He has brought us nigh to God.

Olney parish church, where Newton ministered for nearly sixteen years

Reading and meditation

A Bible Christian

Because I love to read, some of the happiest moments in my life are those rare occasions when I can peruse at my leisure the shelves of an antiquarian bookshop. I love the muted colours of aged leather bindings and the satin feel of well-worn covers. I love the comforting sound of the rustle of antique pages and the quiet murmur of objection that a binding makes when a volume is disturbed for the first time in many years. But I especially love the subtle, musty aroma given off by very old paper. Sometimes I will pick up a book and fan the edges of its pages in front of my face, just for the sheer pleasure of inhaling the book's mellow fragrance. My mother once sent me a newspaper article stating that scientists had discovered that certain spores, which are often found on the paper of old books, had been shown to have a hallucinogenic effect when inhaled in sufficient quantities. She joked that she had discovered the real reason that I loved second-hand bookshops!

Newton also loved to read and understood the power of books for good and for evil. According to his autobiography, he was able to read 'any common book' by the age of four and began his study of Latin with his mother when he was only six — a course of study that was cut short by her death just before his seventh birthday. His education at boarding school, while not a happy experience, advanced his knowledge of Latin and by the time he was ten years old he could read authors like Virgil.

When he was twelve or thirteen years of age, Newton read a book entitled *Characteristics*, which was by a deist, Lord Shaftesbury (1671-1713). The book was seldom out of Newton's hand and its clever, religious-sounding words had a toxic spiritual effect like that of 'a slow poison, and prepared the way for all [his sinful life] that followed'.

As a Christian, Newton attests to the beneficial impact of spiritual literature on his own heart. In a list of his reading prior to entering the ministry, he mentions his appreciation of the works of men such as Matthew Henry, John Wesley, Ralph Erskine and Philip Doddridge. In a letter to a fellow minister, Newton refers to John Owen's *Discourse on the Holy Spirit* as the 'epitome, if not the masterpiece, of his writings'. He thought so highly of this work that he wished to see it reprinted. In that same letter, he also expresses his admiration for Jonathan Edwards' work on the free will of man.[1]

In the excerpts that follow, Newton balances his strong affirmation of the place of books in stimulating spiritual growth with an equally strong reminder (for confessed 'bibliophiles' like myself!) of the superiority and sufficiency of the Word of God over every book of human origin.

Books and letters written in a proper spirit, may, if the Lord is pleased to smile upon them, have their use; but an awakened mind that thirsts after the Saviour, and seeks wisdom by reading and praying over the Scripture, has little occasion for a library of human writings. The Bible is the fountain from whence every stream that deserves our notice is drawn; and, though we may occasionally pay some attention to the streams, we have personally an equal right with others to apply immediately to the fountain-head, and draw the water of life for ourselves. The purest streams are not wholly freed from … a twang [i.e. a trace] of the soil through which they run; a mixture of human infirmity is inseparable from the best human composition, but in the fountain the truth is unmixed…

Books that have a savour and unction may likewise be helpful, provided we read them with caution, compare

them with the Scripture, and do not give ourselves impli-
citly to the rules or decisions of any man or set of men, but
remember that one is our Master and infallible Teacher,
even Christ. But the chief and grand means of edification,
without which all other helps will disappoint us, and prove
like clouds without water, are the Bible and prayer, the
word of grace and the throne of grace. A frequent perusal of
the Bible will give us an enlarged and comprehensive view
of the whole of religion, its origin, nature, genius, and tendency, and preserve us from an over-attachment to any
system of man's compilation. The fault of the several sys-
tems under which, as under so many banners, the different
denominations of Christians are ranged is that there is usually something left out which ought to have been taken in,
and something admitted, of supposed advantage, not authorized by the scriptural standard. A Bible Christian, therefore, will see much to approve in a variety of forms and
parties; the providence of God may lead or fix him in a
more immediate connection with some one of them, but his
spirit and affection will not be confined within these narrow
enclosures. He insensibly borrows and unites that which is
excellent in each, perhaps without knowing how far he
agrees with them, because he finds all in the written Word.

(*Miscellaneous Papers extracted from Periodical Publications,*
'On Reading the Bible')

We may grow wise apace in opinions by books and men;
but vital, experimental knowledge can only be received
from the Holy Spirit, the great instructor of his people... The
Word of God affords a history in miniature of the heart of
man, the devices of Satan, the state of the world, and the
method of grace...

(*Cardiphonia*, 'Six Letters to the Rev. Mr B...', Letter 3)

It is far from my intention to depreciate the value or deny the usefulness of books, without exception: a few well-chosen treatises, carefully perused and thoroughly digested, will deserve and reward our pains; but a multiplicity of reading is seldom attended with a good effect...

Perhaps no country has abounded so much with religious books as our own: many of them are truly excellent; but a very great number of those which are usually more obvious to be met with, as they stand recommended by great names, and the general taste of the public, are more likely to mislead an enquirer than to direct him into the paths of true peace and wisdom.

Here [in the Scriptures] we may seek (and we shall not seek in vain) wherein to combat and vanquish every spiritual error, to illustrate and confirm every spiritual truth. Here are promises suited to every want, direction adapted to every doubt that can possibly arise. Here is milk for babes, meat for strong men, medicines for the wounded, refreshment for the weary. The general history of all nations and ages, and the particular experience of each private believer, from the beginning to the end of time, are wonderfully comprised in this single volume; so that whoever reads and improves it aright [i.e. makes a right use of it], may discover his state, his progress, his temptations, his danger, and his duty, as distinctly and minutely marked out as if the whole had been written for him alone. In this respect, as well as in many others, great is the mystery of godliness...

The simplicity, as well as the subject matter, of the Bible evidences its divine original. Though it has depths sufficient to embarrass and confound the proudest efforts of unsanctified reason, it does not, as to its general import, require an elevated genius to understand it, but is equally addressed to every capacity...

The language of the Bible is likewise clothed with inimitable majesty and authority. God speaks in it, and reveals the glory of his perfections, his sovereignty, holiness, justice, goodness, and grace in a manner worthy of himself, though at the same time admirably adapted to our weakness. The most laboured efforts of human genius are flat and languid, in comparison of those parts of the Bible which are designed to give us due apprehensions of the God with whom we have to do. Where shall we find such instances of the true sublime, the great, the marvellous, the beautiful, the pathetic [i.e. that which appeals to the emotions], as in the Holy Scriptures? Again, the effects which it performs demonstrate it to be the Word of God. With a powerful and penetrating energy, it alarms and pierces the conscience, discovers the thoughts and intents of the heart, convinces the most obstinate, and makes the careless tremble. With equal authority and efficacy, its speaks peace to the troubled mind, heals the wounded spirit, and can impart a joy unspeakable and full of glory, in the midst of the deepest distress. It teaches, persuades, comforts, and reproves, with an authority that can neither be disputed nor evaded; and often communicates more light, motives, and influence by a single sentence to a plain, unlettered believer than he could derive from the voluminous commentaries of the learned. In a word, it answers the character the apostle gives it: 'It is able to make us wise to salvation; it is completely and alone sufficient to make the man of God perfect, thoroughly furnished for every good work.' The doctrines, prophecies, promises, precepts, exhortations, examples, and warnings contained in the Bible form a perfect *whole*, a complete summary of the will of God concerning us, in which nothing is wanting, nothing is superfluous.

(*Forty-One Letters on Religious Subjects*, Letter 15)

The Spirit of God teaches and enlightens by his Word as the instrument. There is no revelation from him, but what is (as to our perception of it) derived from the Scripture. There may be supposed illuminations of, and strong impressions upon, the mind, in which the Word of God has no place or concern; but this [fact] alone is sufficient to discountenance them, and to prove that they are not from the Holy Spirit.

For the Scripture is the appointed rule and test by which all our searches and discoveries, all our acquisitions in religious knowledge, must be tried. If they are indeed from God, they will stand this trial, and answer to the Word, as face answers to face in a glass, but not otherwise. 'To the law and to the testimony, if they speak not according to this word, it is because there is no light in them' [Isaiah 8:20]…

Set a high value upon the Word of God. All that is necessary to make you wise to salvation is there, and there only. In this precious book you may find a direction for every doubt, a solution of every difficulty, a promise suited to every circumstance you can be in. There you may be informed of your disease by sin, and the remedy provided by grace. You may be instructed to know yourselves, to know God and Jesus Christ, in the knowledge of whom standeth eternal life. The wonders of redeeming love, the glories of the Redeemer's person, the happiness of the redeemed people, the power of faith, and the beauty of holiness are here represented to the life. Nothing is wanting [i.e. lacking] to make life useful and comfortable, death safe and desirable, and to bring down something of heaven upon earth. But this true wisdom can be found nowhere else. If you wander from the Scripture, in pursuit either of present peace or future hope, your search will end in disappointment. This is the fountain of living waters; if you forsake it, and give preference to broken cisterns of your own devising, they will fail you when you most need them. Rejoice, therefore that such a treasure is put into your hand.

(*Twenty Sermons Preached in the Parish Church of Olney*,
Sermon 4)

S uggested **Scripture readings:** Nehemiah 8:1-18; 2 Peter
1:2-4

> 'The words of the LORD are pure words; as silver tried in a furnace
> on the earth, refined seven times' (Ps.12:6).

On reading the Scriptures

The advice given here on the reading of Scripture is tempered with
Newton's humble confession of the ever-present temptation to
neglect the precious gift of reading and meditation on God's Word.

I know not a better rule of reading the Scripture than to
read it through from beginning to end and, when we have
finished it once, to begin it again. We shall meet with many
passages which we can make little improvement of [i.e.
from which we can profit little], but not so many in the second reading as in the first, and fewer in the third than in the
second — provided we pray to him who has the keys to
open our understandings, and to anoint our eyes with his
spiritual ointment. The course of reading today will prepare
some lights for what we shall read tomorrow, and throw a
farther light upon what we read yesterday. Experience only
can prove the advantage of this method, if steadily perse-
vered in. To make a few efforts and then give over is like
making a few steps and then standing still, which would do
little towards completing a long journey. But, though a person walked slowly, and but a little way in a day, if he
walked every day, and with his face always in the same
direction, year after year, he might in time encompass the
globe. By thus travelling patiently and steadily through the
Scripture, and repeating our progress, we should increase in

knowledge to the end of life. The Old and New Testament, the doctrines, precepts, and promises, the history, the examples, admonitions, and warnings, etc. would mutually illustrate and strengthen each other, and nothing that is written for our instruction would be overlooked. Happy should I be, could I fully follow the advice I am now offering to you. I wish you may profit by my experience. Alas, how much time have I lost and wasted, which, had I been wise, I should have devoted to reading and studying the Bible! But my evil heart obstructs the dictates of my judgement; I often feel a reluctance to read this book of books, and a disposition to hew out broken cisterns which afford me no water, while the fountain of living waters [is] close within my reach.

(*Miscellaneous Papers extracted from Periodical Publications*, 'On Reading the Bible')

He [a typical believer] takes up the Bible, conscious that it is the fountain of life and true comfort; yet perhaps, while he is making the reflection, he feels a secret distaste, which prompts him to lay it down, and give his preference to a newspaper.

(*Cardiphonia*, 'Twenty-six Letters to a Nobleman', Letter 2)

The Bible, or the New Testament, is frequently used at school, as a school-book; and children often think no more of it than just to read their appointed lesson. But I hope you will consider it as God's book, and when you take it in hand, open it with reverence, and read it with attention, as you think you would if you expected to hear an audible voice from heaven. The plainest and most affecting part of the Bible is the history of our Saviour in the evangelists [i.e. the four Gospels]: read it often, that you may be well acquainted with it. I pray him to enable you to understand what you read. Surely when you read who he is, what he did, what he suffered, and what he has promised poor sinners, you will, you must, love him. And if you once love him, you will study to please him.

(*Letters intended as a Sequel to Cardiphonia*, 'Twenty-One Letters to Miss ...', Letter 20)

The first requisite [to understanding the passage of Scripture that we read] is *sincerity*; I mean the real desire to be instructed by the Scripture, and to submit both our sentiments and our practices to be controlled and directed by what we read there. Without this, our reading and searching will only issue in our greater condemnation, and bring us under the heavy doom of the servant who knew his master's will and did it not...

A second thing is *diligence*... The best understanding is to keep his commandments ... but as we cannot keep them unless we know them, neither can we know them without a diligent enquiry. The word rendered 'search' [from John 5:39, 'Search the scriptures...' (AV)], is borrowed from the practice of miners; it implies two things: to dig and to examine. First, with much labour they pierce the earth to a considerable depth; and [second] when they have thus found a vein of precious ore, they break and sift it, and suffer no part to escape their notice. Thus we must join frequent, assiduous reading with close and awakened meditation; comparing spiritual things with spiritual, carefully taking notice of the circumstances, occasion, and application of what we read; being assured that there is a treasure of truth and happiness under our hands, if we have but the skill to discover and improve it [i.e. profit from it]...

Humility is the third thing very necessary to a profitable perusal of the Scriptures. Let us aim at a humble spirit; let us reflect much on the majesty and grandeur of the God we serve; let us adore his condescension in favouring us with a revelation of his will; let us consider the Word of God and the wisdom of God as terms of the same import; in a word, let us study to know ourselves, our own sinfulness and ignorance; then we shall no longer read the Scriptures with indifference or prepossession, but with the greatest reverence and attention, and with the most enlarged expectation.

(*Six Discourses as Intended for the Pulpit*, Sermon 5)

*S*uggested **Scripture readings**: Psalm 19:7-14; 119:25-32

'*You search the Scriptures because you think that in them you have eternal life*' (John 5:39).

Using the law 'lawfully'

Have you ever wondered about where the Old Testament law fits into your life as a New Testament Christian? Should you attempt to keep the Ten Commandments, or ignore them? How you answer that simple question places you on one side or the other of a thorny theological debate that has separated churches and denominations throughout history. In the letter below, Newton states that, with regard to a believer and the law, there are, in general, two errors to be avoided. The first is to attempt to 'use [the law] to seek justification and acceptance with God by our obedience to it'. The second is 'to pretend that [the accomplishment of the law] by Christ releases believers from any obligation to it as a rule'. In a wonderfully concise way, Newton summarizes this complex, but important issue of the 'lawful' use of the law.

You desire my thoughts on I Timothy 1:8, 'We know that the law is good if a man use it lawfully,' and I willingly comply... Ignorance of the nature and design of the law is at the bottom of most religious mistakes... If we [look at] what is meant by the law and by what means we know the law to be good, I think it will ... be easy to conclude what it is to use the law lawfully...

The law of God ... in the largest sense, is that rule, or prescribed course, which he has appointed for his creatures ... that they may answer the end for which he has created them...

The Decalogue, or ten commands, uttered by the voice of God himself, is an abstract [i.e. a summary] of that original law under which man was created... This law could not be designed as a covenant, by obedience to which man should be justified...

To this was superadded the ceremonial or Levitical law... Both [Old and New Testament believers] renounce any dependence on the moral law for justification, and both accept it as a rule of life ... and are enabled to yield it a sincere, though not a perfect, obedience.

A second enquiry is, how we came to know the law to be good. For naturally we do not, we cannot think so. We cannot be at enmity with God and at the same time approve of his law; rather this is the ground of our dislike to him that we conceive the law by which we are judged is too strict in its precepts, and too severe in its threatenings...

These prejudices against the law can only be removed by the power of the Holy Spirit. It is his office to enlighten and convince the conscience; to communicate an impression of the majesty, holiness, justice and authority of the God with whom we have to do. It is his office likewise to discover the grace and glory of the Saviour, as having fulfilled the law for us... Then a change of judgement takes place, and the sinner consents to the law, that it is holy, just, and good. Then the law is acknowledged to be holy: it manifests the holiness of God...

We may now proceed to enquire, in the last place, what it is to use the law lawfully...

The law is lawfully used as a means of conviction of sin: for this purpose it was promulgated at Sinai. The law entered, that sin might abound ... to make [sinful men] sensible [i.e. aware] how wicked they are. Having God's law in our hands, we are no longer to form our judgements by the maxims and customs of the world, where evil is called good, and good evil; but are to try [i.e. test] every principle, temper and practice, by this standard...

Again, when we use the law as a glass to behold the glory of God, we use it lawfully. His glory is eminently revealed in Christ... We see the perfection and excellence of the law in his life. God was glorified by his obedience as a man. What a perfect character did he exhibit! Yet it is no other than a transcript of the law...

Another lawful use ... is to consult it as a rule and pattern by which to regulate our spirit and conversation [i.e. lifestyle]. The grace of God, received by faith, will dispose us to obedience in general, but ... we are much at a loss as to particulars. We are therefore sent to the law, that we may learn how to walk worthy of God, who has called us to his kingdom and glory; and every precept has its proper place and use.

Lastly, we use the law lawfully when we improve [i.e. use] it as a test whereby to judge of the exercise of grace. Believers differ so much from what they once were ... that without this right use of the law, comparing themselves with their former selves, or with others, they would be prone to think more highly of their attainments than they ought. But when they recur to [the high standard of the law], they sink into the dust, and adopt the language of Job: 'Behold, I am vile; I cannot answer thee, one of a thousand' [Job 40:3; 9:3, AV].

From hence we may collect [i.e. conclude] in brief how the law is good to them that use it lawfully. It furnishes them with a comprehensive and accurate view of the will

of God, and the path of duty. By the study of the law they
acquire an habitual spiritual taste of what is right and
wrong… [The law] likewise, by reminding them of their
deficiencies and shortcomings, is a sanctified means of
making and keeping them humble; and it exceedingly en-
dears Jesus, the law-fulfiller, to their hearts, and puts them
in mind of their obligations to him, and of their absolute
dependence upon him every moment.

(*Forty-One Letters on Religious Subjects*, Letter 30)

S uggested **Scripture readings:** Romans 3:21-31; Galatians
3:6-22; 1 Timothy 1:3-11

> '*But we know that the law is good, if one uses it lawfully*'
> (I Tim. 1:8).

Listening to sermons

Newton's preaching, like his path to the pulpit, was far from typical.
Richard Cecil, a close friend, ardent admirer and biographer of
Newton, said of his preaching, 'With respect to his ministry, he
appeared, perhaps, at least advantage in the pulpit, as he did not
generally aim at accuracy in the composition of his sermons, nor at
any address in the delivery of them. His utterance was far from
clear, and his attitudes ungraceful. He possessed, however, so much
affection for his people, and much zeal for their best interest, that
the defect of his manner was of little consideration with his constant
hearers; at the same time, his capacity and habit of entering into
their trials and experience gave the highest interest to his ministry
among them. Besides which he frequently interspersed the most
brilliant allusions, and brought forward such happy illustrations of
his subject, and those with so much unction on his own heart, as
melted and enlarged theirs. The parent-like tenderness and affection

which accompanied his instruction made them prefer him to preachers who, on other accounts, were much more generally popular.'[2]

God blessed Newton's pulpit ministry with many conversions. Thirteen months after his arrival in Olney, a gallery was constructed in order to accommodate the swelling congregation. Several years later, not long after his move to London, the congregation of St Mary Woolnoth experienced the same phenomenon. A church official at St Mary's proposed that if Newton were from time to time to preach elsewhere, without notice, so that the congregation could never be sure of his presence, the number of visitors might be reduced.[3] Instead, as in Olney, a gallery was built for additional seating. Whatever may have been lacking in Newton's unique, unpretentious style of preaching, there were many who were thriving under his ministry.

The following excerpts contain penetrating advice from this most distinctive preacher, not on preaching, but on listening to sermons. His counsel focuses on two fronts: first, the necessity of not only being a hearer but a doer of the Word; and, second, being sure to put all sermons to the litmus test of Scripture itself.

In the first place, be cautious that you do not degenerate into the spirit of a *mere hearer*, so as to place the chief stress of your profession upon running hither and thither after preachers. There are many who ... seem to think that they were sent into this world only to hear sermons, and to hear as many in a day as they possibly can... If the twelve apostles were again upon earth, and you could hear them all every week, yet, if you were not attentive to the duties of the closet [i.e. private prayer], if you did not allow yourself time for reading, meditation, and prayer ... I should be more ready to blame your indiscretion than to admire your zeal. No public ordinances can make amends for the neglect of secret prayer; nor will the most diligent attendance upon them justify us in the neglect of those duties which, by the command and appointment of God, we owe to society.

Newton's pulpit at the church of St Mary Woolnoth

Again, as it is our trial to live in a day wherein so many contentions and winds of strange doctrine abound, I hope you will watch and pray that you may not have itching ears, inclining you to hearken after novel and singular opinions, and the erroneous sentiments of men of unstable minds, who are not sound in the faith. I have known persons who, from a blameable curiosity, have gone to hear [preachers of strange doctrines], not for the sake of edification, which they could not expect, but to know what they had to say, supposing that they themselves were too well established in the truth to be hurt, yea, many have been overthrown. Error is like poison; the subtleness, quickness, and force of its operation [are] often amazing… If the Lord has shown you what is right, it is not worth your while to know (if you could know it) how many ways there are to be wrong.

Farther, I advise you, when you hear a gospel sermon, and it is not in all respects to your satisfaction, be not too hasty to lay the whole blame upon the preacher… Indeed … it will be more useful to you, who are a hearer, to consider whether the fault may not possibly be in yourself. Perhaps you thought too highly of the man, and expected too much from him; or perhaps you thought too meanly of him [i.e. you had too low an opinion of him] and expected too little. In the former case, the Lord justly disappointed you; and in the latter, you received according to your faith. Perhaps you neglected to pray for [the preacher]; and then, though he might be useful to others, it is not at all strange that he was not so to you. Or possibly you have indulged a trifling spirit, and brought a dearth and deadness upon your soul, for which you have not been duly humbled, and the Lord chose that time to rebuke you.

Lastly, as a hearer, you have a right to try [i.e. test] all doctrines by the Word of God, and it is your duty so to do. Faithful ministers will remind you of this: they do not wish to hold you in an implicit and blind obedience to what they say, upon their own authority, nor desire that you should follow them farther than they have the Scripture for their warrant. They would not be lords over your conscience, but helpers of your joy. Prize this gospel liberty, which sets you free from the doctrines and commandments of men; but do not abuse it to the purposes of pride and self. There are hearers who make *themselves*, and not the Scripture, the standard of their judgement. They attend not so much to be instructed, as to pass their sentence. To them, the pulpit is the bar at which the minister stands to take his trial before them — a bar at which few escape censure, from judges at once so severe and inconsistent... These censors are not all of a mind, and perhaps agree in nothing so much as in the opinion they have of their own wisdom.

Oh, this is a hateful spirit, that prompts hearers to pronounce *ex cathedra* [i.e. in an authoritative manner] as if they were infallible, [that] breaks in upon the rights of private judgement, even in matters not essential, and makes a man an offender by a word! This spirit is one frequent unhappy evil which springs from the corruption of the heart, when the Lord affords the means of grace in abundance. How highly would some of the Lord's hidden ones [those in remote places], who are destitute of the ordinances, prize the blessing of a preached gospel, with which too many professors seem to be surfeited [i.e. to have had more than enough]! I pray God to preserve you from such a spirit (which I fear is spreading and infects us like pestilence), and to guide you in all things.

(Forty-one Letters on Religious Subjects, Letter 13)

And as this doctrine [justification by faith alone, in Christ alone] is of so great and essential importance, beware how you listen to any other. Take heed how you hear [Mark 4:24; Luke 8:18]; be not influenced by the names, characters, or stations [i.e. rank] of men, when the salvation of your souls is at stake. Prize the liberty which ... you enjoy, of bringing every doctrine to the trial of God's Word, and freely use it. I account it my honour and happiness that I preach to a free people, who have the Bible in their hands; to your Bible I appeal. I entreat, I charge you to receive nothing upon my word, any farther than I prove it from the Word of God; and bring every preacher, and every sermon that you hear, to the same standard. If this is the truth, you had need to be well established in it; for it is not the current and fashionable doctrine of the times. Let me recommend farther to you (it is a directive our Lord has given), to examine doctrines by their effects: 'By their fruits ye shall know them' [Matthew 7:16]. The truths of God, when faithfully preached, in humble dependence upon his blessing, will be attested by his power. At such times, and in such places, a visible change will soon be observable in some or more of the hearers; they cease to do evil, they learn to do well; they acknowledge God in all their ways, and glorify him before men, by living according to his precepts. And if you ask them the reason for this change, they will freely ascribe it to the blessing of God upon that sort of preaching, which by too many is accounted as foolishness [1 Corinthians 1:21].

(*Twenty Sermons Preached at Olney*, Sermon 18)

I think hearers should be careful not to be prejudiced against a doctrine, merely because it is not well supported; for perhaps it is capable of solid proof, though the preacher was not so happy as to hit upon that which was most suitable; and extempore preachers [i.e. those who preach without a written text of their sermon] may sometimes hope for a little allowance upon this head, from the more candid part of their auditory, and not be made offenders for an inadvertence which they cannot perhaps always avoid in the hurry of speaking.

(*Cardiphonia*, 'Seven Letters to Mrs ...', Letter 2)

*S*uggested **Scripture readings:** Acts 17:10-12; 2 Timothy 4:1-4; James 1:19-27

> *'But prove yourselves doers of the word, and not merely hearers who delude themselves'* (James 1:22).

The Word as a sword

The two hymns quoted below both describe the Word of God as a piercing sword, but in radically different ways. In the first hymn Scripture is described as a blade in the hand of Christ that slices with the precision of a surgeon's knife, exposing the hidden motives of men's hearts. How sobering and convicting to be reminded that our souls stand 'naked, without disguise' before the Lord's 'all-piercing eyes', and that he will never be pleased with righteous actions that come from impure motives! The Lord insists that we not only do the right thing, but that we do it for the right reason. In other words, our motives *do* matter. Newton then goes on to comfort us with the knowledge that Christ's omniscience is not limited only to the secret sins of our hearts, but that he also knows our hearts' secret fears and hears our unspoken prayers. What a powerful instrument is the Word of Christ, equally able to convict or to comfort, according to the need of the moment!

The Word quick and powerful
Hebrews 4:12-13

*T*he word of Christ, our Lord,
  With whom we have to do,
Is sharper than a two-edged sword,
To pierce a sinner through!

Swift as the lightning's blaze
When awful thunders roll,

It fills the conscience with amaze [i.e. amazement],
And penetrates the soul.

No heart can be concealed
From his all-piercing eyes;
Each thought and purpose stands revealed,
Naked, without disguise.

He sees his people's fears;
He notes their mournful cry;
He counts their sighs and falling tears,
And helps them from on high.

Though feeble is their good,
It has his kind regard;
Yea, all they would do, if they could,
Shall find a sure reward.

He sees the wicked too,
And will repay them soon,
For all the evil deeds they do,
And all they would have done.

Since all our secret ways
Are marked and known by thee;
Afford us, Lord, thy light of grace
That we ourselves may see.

(Olney Hymns, Book 1, Hymn 133)

In this second hymn, the Bible is again referred to as a weapon, but in this text the sword is not the one wielded by the Lord, but by each believer, and it is not the Christian's heart, but the Christian's enemy, that is to be pierced by Scripture's cutting edge. This song speaks of that sword which is a part of the Christian soldier's armour — the sword of the Spirit. The Scriptures are designed to overcome

Satan and his hosts, who, with lies, threats and temptations, wage war against our souls.

The Word more precious than gold

*P*recious Bible! What a treasure
    Does the Word of God afford!
All I want for life or pleasure,
Food and medicine, shield and sword:
Let the world account me poor,
Having this, I need no more.

Food to which the world's a stranger,
Here my hungry soul enjoys;
Of excess there is no danger,
Though it fills, it never cloys [i.e. gluts]:
On a dying Christ I feed;
He is meat and drink indeed!

When my faith is faint and sickly,
Or when Satan wounds my mind,
Cordials, to revive me quickly,
Healing medicines here I find:
To the promises I flee;
Each affords a remedy.

In the hour of dark temptation
Satan cannot make me yield;
For the word of consolation
Is to me a mighty shield;
While the Scripture truths are sure,
From his malice I'm secure.

Vain his threats to overcome me,
When I take the Spirit's sword;
Then with ease I drive him from me.

Satan trembles at the Word:
'Tis a sword for conquest made,
Keen the edge, and strong the blade.

Shall I envy then the miser,
Doting on his golden store?
Sure I am, or should be, wiser,
I am rich; 'tis he is poor:
Jesus gives me, in his Word,
Food and medicine, shield and sword.

(Olney Hymns, Book 2, Hymn 63)

S **uggested Scripture readings:** Hebrews 4:11-16; Ephesians 6:10-18; Psalm 119:9-16,89-96

> *'For the word of God is living and active and sharper than any two-edged sword, and piercing as far as the division of soul and spirit, of both joints and marrow, and able to judge the thoughts and intentions of the heart'* (Heb. 4:12).

Prayer

Weakness in prayer

When it came to his personal prayer life, Newton was himself a bundle of contradictions — the kind of contradictions that endear him to us, because they remind us so much of ourselves. While he firmly believed in the power of prayer, he admitted to struggling greatly with the practice of prayer. Newton's honesty about his battle to maintain his prayer life, both 'secret' and public, is mentioned frequently in his letters and hymns. In the selections quoted below I have found comfort that even a great man of God like Newton had to battle with distractions and 'backwardness' in prayer. I can relate all too well to his statements about perceiving prayer as a task and a chore rather than a joy and privilege. But in addition to deriving comfort from Newton's candour, I am also warned against the temptation to sin by speaking publicly of my own prayer life in a way that would leave an impression that it is stronger or more consistent than it is in reality. I agree with Newton that, of all the spiritual disciplines, private prayer is certainly among the most neglected and resisted by our lazy flesh.

Many a prayer I have put [i.e. sent] up for you, since I saw you. I hope the Lord will answer us for ourselves and each other. I hope that you will not be wanting [i.e. will not fail] to pray for yourself. Prayer is the great secret which gives true relish to life. When I can pray with some liberty, I find all goes on well; when I cannot, I have no real pleasure in anything. I believe I should not have begun my letter in so complaining a strain [concerning the delays of the postal service and his great loneliness in missing his wife], if I was not much out of frame [i.e. the right state of mind] for prayer. 'Draw nigh to God and he will draw nigh to you,' is a maxim that we ought always to regard.

(*Letters to a Wife*, Letter dated 'Liverpool, August 6, 1760')

I look upon prayer meetings as the most profitable exercises (excepting the public preaching) in which Christians can engage; they have a direct tendency to kill a worldly, trifling spirit, to draw down a divine blessing upon all our concerns, compose differences, and enkindle (at least to maintain) the flame of divine love amongst brethren. But I need not tell you the advantages; you know them: I only would exhort you; and the rather as I find in my own case the principal cause of my leanness and unfruitfulness is owing to an unaccountable backwardness to pray. I can write, or read, or converse, or hear, with a ready will; but prayer is more spiritual and inward than any of these; and the more spiritual any duty is, the more my carnal heart is apt to start from it. May the Lord pour forth his precious spirit of prayer and supplication in both our hearts.

(*Cardiphonia*, 'Eight Letters to the Rev. Mr ...,' Letter 8)

Thoughts on prayer from Newton's hymns[4]

*H*e bids me always freely come,
   And promises whate'er I ask;
But I am straitened [i.e. under constraint], cold and dumb,
And count my privilege a task.

(*Olney Hymns*, Book 1, Hymn 30)

Thy saints are comforted, I know,
And love thy house of prayer;

I therefore go where others go,
But find no comfort there.

(*Olney Hymns*, Book 1, Hymn 64)

Could my heart so hard remain,
Prayer a task and burden prove,
Every trifle give me pain,
If I knew a Saviour's love?

(*Olney Hymns*, Book 1, Hymn 119)

I know the Lord is nigh,
And would, but cannot, pray;
For Satan meets me when I try,
And frights my soul away.

(*Olney Hymns*, Book 1, Hymn 126)

I prize the privilege of prayer,
But oh, what backwardness to pray!
Though on the Lord I cast my care,
I feel its burden every day:
I seek his will in all I do,
Yet find my own is working too.

(*Olney Hymns*, Book 1, Hymn 130)

If I attempt to pray,
And lisp thy holy name;
My thoughts are hurried soon away,
I know not where I am.

(*Olney Hymns*, Book 3, Hymn 7)

Sure the Lord thus far has brought me
By his watchful tender care;
Sure 'tis he himself has taught me
How to seek his face by prayer:
Will he give me up at last?

(*Olney Hymns*, Book 3, Hymn 52)

O my Lord, what shall I say?
How can I presume to pray?
Not a word have I to plead,
Sins, like mine, are black indeed!

(*Olney Hymns*, Book 3, Hymn 76)

Suggested Scripture readings: Romans 8:26-34; Hebrews
7:25

---

*'Pray to your Father who is in secret, and your Father who sees
what is done in secret will reward you'* (Matt. 6:6).

Power in prayer

While Newton freely admitted that believers are often reluctant to
pray, the following excerpts affirm that God is never reluctant to
answer. Newton encouraged his readers and hearers that the
ultimate motivation to pray, and the confidence that God will
answer, must be grounded in the character of God. His words
remind us that the Lord's ear is always attentive, that his eye is
always watchful, that his hand is always mighty to intervene and
that he will never disappoint us. Reminders of these truths combat
the subtle doubt that sometimes creeps into our hearts that, while
God possesses the power to answer our prayers, he may or may not
be *willing* to do so. How sweet to know that we do not cry out to a
disinterested God! He is not only able but also willing, yes even
zealous, to answer our prayers. Be sure to note the references in the
final sermon excerpt, and also in the hymn, to God's mighty answer
to the prayer of Hezekiah (regarding Sennacherib's threats) and to
the prayer of the early church (regarding Peter's deliverance from
prison).

Prayer is indeed the best half of our business while upon
earth, and that which gives spirit and efficacy [i.e. power] to

all the rest. Prayer is not only our immediate duty, but the highest dignity, the richest privilege we are capable of receiving on this side of eternity; and the neglect of it *implies* the deepest guilt and *includes* the heaviest punishment. A stranger to prayer is equally a stranger to God and to happiness, 'like the wave of the sea driven with the wind and tossed' (James 1). Are any of you, my friends, unacquainted with prayer? Then you are without a guide in prosperity, without resource in distress, without true comfort in life, and while you continue so, without hope in death.

(*Six Discourses Intended for the Pulpit*, Sermon 5, 'On Searching the Scriptures')

How little does the world know of that intercourse which is carried on between heaven and earth; what petitions are daily presented, and what answers are received at a throne of grace! Oh, the blessed privilege of prayer! Oh, the wonderful love, care, attention, and power of our great Shepherd! His eye is always upon us; when our spirits are almost overwhelmed within us, he knoweth our path. His ear is always open to us: let who will overlook and disappoint us, he will not. When means and hope fail, when everything looks dark upon us, when we seem shut up on every side, when we are brought to the lowest ebb, still our help is in the name of the Lord who made heaven and earth. To him all things are possible; and before the exertion of his power, when he is pleased to arise and work, all hindrances give way and vanish, like a mist before the sun. And he can so manifest himself to the soul, and cause his goodness to pass before it, that the hour of affliction shall be the golden hour of the greatest consolation.

(*Cardiphonia*, 'Eight Letters to Mrs ...,' Letter 4)

Let us pray in faith. Let us remember what great things the Lord has done in answer to prayer. When sin had given Sennacherib rapid success in his invasion of Judah, he did not know that he was not more than an axe, or a saw, in the hand of God. He ascribed his victories to his own prowess, and thought himself equally sure of Jerusalem. But Hezekiah defeated him upon his knees. He spread his blasphemous letter before the Lord in the temple and prayed; and the Assyrian army melted away like snow. When Peter was shut up, and chained in prison, the chains fell off, the locks and bolts gave way, and the iron gate opened, while the church was united in earnest prayer for his deliverance.

(Sermon entitled, 'The Imminent Danger and the Only Sure Resource of this Nation')

Power of prayer

*I*n themselves, as weak as worms,
How can poor believers stand,
When temptations, foes, and storms
Press them close on every hand?

Weak, indeed, they feel they are,
But they know the throne of grace;
And the God who answers prayer
Helps them when they seek his face.

Though the Lord awhile delay,
Succour they at length obtain;
He who taught their hearts to pray
Will not let them cry in vain.

Wrestling prayer can wonders do,
Bring relief in deepest straits;
Prayer can force a passage through
Iron bars and brazen gates.

Hezekiah on his knees
Proud Assyria's host subdued;
And when smitten with disease,
Had his life by prayer renewed.

Peter, though confined and chained,
Prayer prevailed and brought him out;
When Elijah prayed, it rained,
After three long years of drought.

We can likewise witness bear
That the Lord is still the same;
Though we feared he would not hear,
Suddenly deliverance came.

For the wonders he has wrought,
Let us now our praises give;
And, by sweet experience taught,
Call upon him while we live.

(Olney Hymns, Book 2, Hymn 61)

S **uggested Scripture readings:** Isaiah 37:1-38; Acts 12:1-19

'So Peter was kept in the prison, but prayer for him was being made fervently by the church to God' (Acts 12:5).

Improving your public prayers

Times of corporate prayer were numerous and a vital part of Newton's first ministry in Olney. On Sundays, a group would gather at 6 a.m. to pray for their pastor's ministry that day. Following the morning and afternoon services, a small group would gather in the Newtons' home, after tea, for an hour of singing and prayer. This little home prayer group swelled to seventy and eventually gave rise to an evening service. Newton divided his entire parish into groups of eight to twelve so that he could meet with them to talk and pray once every six weeks. In addition there were specially called times of prayer for various needs or national crises. A regular Tuesday evening prayer meeting, which began with around forty adults, eventually was relocated to Lord Dartmouth's Great House, adjacent to the church, which could accommodate up to 130 persons. The following hymn was written for that occasion:

On opening a place for social prayer

O Lord, our languid souls inspire,
For here, we trust, thou art!
Send down a coal of heavenly fire
To warm each waiting heart.

Dear Shepherd of thy people, hear,
Thy presence now display;
As thou hast given a place for prayer,
So give us hearts to pray.

Show us some token of thy love,
Our fainting hope to raise;
And pour thy blessings from above
That we may render praise.

Within these walls let holy peace,
And love, and concord dwell;
Here give the troubled conscience ease,
The wounded spirit heal.

The feeling heart, the melting eye,
The humble mind bestow;

And shine upon us from on high,
To make our graces grow.

May we in faith receive thy word,
In faith present our prayers;
And, in the presence of the Lord,
Unbosom all our cares.

And may the gospel's joyful sound,
Enforced by mighty grace,
Awaken many sinners round,
To come and fill the place.

(*Olney Hymns*, Book 2, Hymn 43)

Since Newton attended and led so many weekly public gatherings for corporate prayer, he certainly had ample opportunity to evaluate the strengths and weaknesses of various methods of public prayer. He offered the following exceedingly practical advice on how to improve one's public prayers:

The chief fault of some good prayers is that they are too long — not that I think we should pray by the clock, and limit ourselves precisely to a certain number of minutes; but it is better, of the two, that the hearer should wish the prayer had been longer than spend half [of it] or a considerable time wishing it was over... Long prayers should in general be avoided, especially where several persons are to pray successively; or else even spiritual hearers will be unable to keep up their attention...

Prayer should be sententious [i.e. heartfelt], and made up of breathings to the Lord, either of confession, petition, or praise. It should be not only scriptural and evangelical, but experimental — a simple and unstudied expression of the wants and feelings of the soul. It will be so if the heart is lively and affected in its duty...

We often find that unlettered [i.e. uneducated] people, who have had little or no help from books [i.e. set prayers, as in the Prayer Book], or rather have not been fettered by them, can pray with an unction and savour in an unpremeditated way, while the prayers of ministers themselves are, though accurate and regular, so dry and starched that they afford little either of pleasure or profit to a spiritual mind.

Many, perhaps most, people who pray in public have some favourite word or expression, which recurs too often in their prayers ... having no connection with the sense of what they are speaking. The most disagreeable of these is when the name of the blessed God, with the addition of perhaps one or more epithets, as 'Great', 'Glorious', 'Holy', 'Almighty', etc., is introduced so often, and without necessity, as seems neither to indicate a due reverence in the person who uses it, nor suited to excite reverence in those who hear.

There are several things likewise respecting the voice and manner of prayer, which a person may with due care correct in himself... Very loud speaking is a fault, when the size of the place, and the number of hearers, do not render it necessary. The end [i.e. purpose] of speaking is to be heard; and when that end is attained, a greater elevation of the voice is frequently hurtful to the speaker, and is more likely to confuse a hearer than to fix his attention... The other extreme, of speaking too low, is not so frequent; but if we are not heard, we might as well altogether hold our peace. It exhausts the spirits, and wearies the attention, to be listening for a length of time to a very low voice...

The tone of voice is likewise regarded. Some have a tone in prayer so different from their usual way of speaking that their nearest friends, if not accustomed to them, could hardly know them by their voice... Contrary to this, and still more offensive, is a custom that some have of talking to the Lord in prayer. It is their natural voice, indeed; but it is that expression of it which they use upon the most familiar and trivial occasions... When we speak to the King of kings ... [should not] the consideration of his glory and our own vileness, and of the important concerns we are engaged in before him, impress us with an air of seriousness and reverence, and prevent us from speaking to him as if he was altogether such a one as ourselves? The liberty to which we are called by the gospel does not at all encourage such a pertness and familiarity.

(*Forty-One Letters on Religious Subjects*, Letter 19)

Suggested **Scripture readings:** Matthew 6:5-15; 26:36-46

'*Therefore I want the men in every place to pray, lifting up holy hands, without wrath and dissension*' (1 Tim. 2:8).

Personal worship

My soul, what can you give?

The hymn quoted below contains Newton's reflections on Psalm 116:12-13. In the original psalm, the psalmist sings of his love for the Lord who delivered him from 'the cords of death', 'the terrors of Sheol' and intense 'distress and sorrow'. The psalmist pours out his gratitude to the God who rescued his 'eyes from tears' and his 'feet from stumbling'. In return for God's rich mercy, he asks himself the question: 'What can I give back to God?' The answer is simple: grateful, humble worship. He says, 'I shall lift up the cup of salvation and call upon the name of the LORD.'

Prior to his conversion, Newton was a wicked, slave-trading sailor who was rescued in extraordinary ways from many life-threatening situations: storms at sea, near-drowning, extended exposure to the elements, severe illness, as well as cruel mistreatment while himself a 'slave' in Africa. No doubt the vivid memories of these divine deliverances paraded through Newton's mind as he read this psalm and penned these lyrics. Like the psalmist, he concluded that he possessed nothing that he could offer to God in return for such dramatic interventions except his humble worship. In addition to the sheer gratitude contained in this hymn, notice too the humility expressed in the lines:

Yet would I glory in the thought
That I will owe him most.

Here Newton surely reflects the perspective of every believer —
that, in the light of our great sin and God's even greater grace, each
Christian considers himself or herself the greatest debtor to God.

One of my daughters demonstrated this kind of humility one
night as I was tucking her into bed. 'Daddy,' she asked, 'tell me one
more time what a Christian is.' I replied, 'Honey, the Bible says a
Christian is someone who by God's grace has had their eyes
opened to see that they are a great sinner.' Before I could go on to
say that a Christian is someone who has also been enabled by
God's grace to see that Jesus is a great Saviour and to place their
trust in him, she interrupted me and said, 'Oh Daddy, I've always
believed that! I am the greatest sinner in our whole family.' I
replied, 'No, honey, *I* am the greatest sinner in our family. I have
been alive longer and had more time to practise sinning than you
have.' She remained unconvinced, still believing her sin to be
greater than anyone else's. In the same way, humble-hearted
believers will vie with the apostle Paul for the title 'chief of sinners'
and argue with Newton, 'No, no, no… *I* owe him the most.'

What shall I render?
Psalm 116:12-13

*F*or mercies, countless as the sands,
　　Which daily I receive
From Jesus', my Redeemer's hands,
　　My soul, what canst thou give?

Alas! From such a heart as mine,
　　What can I bring him forth?
My best is stained and dyed with sin;
　　My all is nothing worth.

Yet this acknowledgement I'll make
　　For all he has bestowed:
Salvation's sacred cup I'll take
　　And call upon my God.

The best return for one like me,
So wretched and so poor,
Is from his gifts to draw a plea,
And ask him still for more.

I cannot serve him as I ought;
No works have I to boast;
Yet would I glory in the thought
That I shall owe him most.

(*Olney Hymns*, Book 1, Hymn 50)

The following hymn is noted in the *Olney Hymnal* as having a similar theme to the one above. It also contains a sweet confession of the tremendous debt of love which believers owe to their Lord.

The happy debtor

*T*en thousand talents once I owed,
        And nothing had to pay;
But Jesus freed me from the load,
And washed my debt away.

Yet since the Lord forgave my sin,
And blotted out my score,
Much more indebted I have been
Than e'er I was before.

My guilt is cancelled quite, I know,
And satisfaction made;
But the vast debt of love I owe
Can never be repaid.

The love I owe for sin forgiven,
For power to believe,
For present peace, and promised heaven,
No angel can conceive.

That love of thine, thou sinner's Friend!
Witness thy bleeding heart!
My little all can ne'er extend
To pay a thousandth part.

Nay more, the poor returns I make
I first from thee obtain;
And 'tis of grace, that thou wilt take
Such poor returns again.

'Tis well — it shall my glory be
(Let who will boast their store)
In time and to eternity,
To owe thee more and more.

(*Olney Hymns*, Book 3, Hymn 67)

*S*uggested **Scripture reading:** Psalm 116

'What shall I render to the LORD
For all his benefits toward me?
I shall lift up the cup of salvation,
And call upon the name of the LORD'
(Ps. 116:12-13).

Songs angels cannot sing

These days it seems the whole world has gone crazy over angels. You will often see a cute little angel pinned on someone's lapel, or a chubby, naked cherub gracing someone's bookshelf or mantelpiece. There has even been a popular TV series based on the intervention of angels. However, the Scripture's view of angels is dramatically different from that of the world. In the Bible, angels are never depicted as 'cute'. Instead, they are shown as powerful, intimidating servants of God who perform his will, proclaim his messages and declare his praise, and their appearances to humans were always in a masculine form. Passages like Isaiah 6 and Revelation chapters 4 and 5 depict the unceasing, passionate worship of the angels around the throne of God. Their response to the sight of God's glory is intense and fervent. Their adoration of the Lamb is bold and unreserved. Surely our own worship seems coolly indifferent and shamefully anaemic compared with that of the angels.

The hymn below is one of six in the *Olney Hymnal* written especially for worship at Christmas time. In it Newton points out that the disparity between the angels' worship and our own is especially ironic in the light of the fact that we have so much more to be grateful for than the angels do. When angels sinned just once, they were immediately judged by God and given no opportunity of redemption (2 Peter 2:4; Jude 6). Yet wicked humans, whose sins are so many and so great, are offered forgiveness through Jesus Christ. So, while the angels declare that the Lamb of God is worthy to be praised, they are merely objectively proclaiming the fact of his worthiness. However, when redeemed sinners like us worship the Lamb, our involvement is intensely personal. We praise the Lamb not merely because he suffered and was slain, but because he suffered for *our* sin and was slain for *us*! Since the angels have less to praise God for than we do, let us at the very least match their intensity in our worship now and look forward to a time in heaven when we might actually surpass them in our praise around the throne.

Man honoured above angels

*N*ow let us join with hearts and tongues,
And emulate the angels' songs;
Yea, sinners may address their King
In songs the angels cannot sing.

They praise the Lamb who once was slain,
But we can add a higher strain,
Not only say, 'He suffered thus,'
But that he suffered all for *us*.

When angels by transgression fell,
Justice consigned them all to hell;
But mercy formed a wondrous plan,
To save, and honour fallen man.

Jesus, who passed the angels by,
Assumed our flesh to bleed and die;
And still he makes it his abode;
As man he fills the throne of God.

Our next of kin, our Brother now,
Is he to whom the angels bow;
They join with us to praise his name,
But *we* the nearest interest claim.

But, ah, how faint our praises rise!
Sure, 'tis the wonder of the skies
That we, who share his richest love,
So cold and unconcerned should prove.

Oh, glorious hour! It comes with speed!
When we, from sin and darkness freed,
Shall see the God who died for man,
And praise him more than angels can.

(*Olney Hymns,* Book 2, Hymn 39)

S uggested Scripture readings: Isaiah 6:1-8; 1 Peter 1:10-12

> '... these things ... have now been announced to you through those
> who preached the gospel to you by the Holy Spirit sent from heaven
> — things into which angels long to look' (1 Peter 1:12).

The song of the redeemed

The sermon quoted below on the worship of heaven was one of a series of fifty topical messages that Newton preached in London in 1784–1785 on the passages of Scripture set to music by Handel in his famous oratorio *Messiah*. They were delivered in conjunction with the placing of a memorial to Handel in Westminster Abbey and a series of performances of the *Messiah*. Newton stated in the first of these messages:

> Conversation, in almost every company, for some time past, has much turned upon the commemoration of Handel... I apprehend that true Christians, without the assistance of either vocal or instrumental music, may find greater pleasure in a humble contemplation of the *words* of the *Messiah* than they can derive from the utmost efforts of musical genius... I mean to lead your meditations to the language of the oratorio, and to consider in their order ... the several sublime and interesting passages of Scripture which are the basis of that admired composition.
>
> (*Fifty sermons on Handel's 'The Messiah'*, Sermon 1)

This particular sermon (and the hymn which follows) is based on Revelation 5:9. This passage is one of those places in the Scriptures in which we are privileged to 'eavesdrop' on the perfect worship of heaven. In it, we hear the lyrics of the majestic song sung by the courts of heaven in praise of the worthiness of the Lamb for his purchase for God of men from every nation with his own blood.

Someone has rightly said that the word 'wonder' is a great synonym for worship. When we contemplate God's goodness, which is lavished on us in Jesus, we do indeed wonder. Sometimes in corporate or private worship we experience answers to our spiritual questions, but at other times, worship seems to create more questions than it answers. Worship can leave us wondering, 'Why does God love me?', or 'Why should Christ endure agony for me?', or 'Why did God quicken my conscience and awaken me from my spiritual indifference?' Questions of this kind are of the very essence of worship. The 'shock and awe' that each of us feels, when we consider God's majestic holiness, the offensiveness of our vile sinful hearts and God's undeserved mercy, grace and love shown to us in Christ Jesus, are characteristic of the wonder of true worship. As Newton admonishes, let the worship of heaven begin with us — now!

> But though this song, and this joy, will only be consummated in heaven, the commencement takes place upon earth. Believers, during their present state of warfare, are taught to sing it; in feebler stains indeed, but the subject of their joy, and the object of their praise, are the same which inspire the harps and songs in the world of light. May I not say that this life is the time of their rehearsal? They are now learning their song, and advancing in meetness [i.e. becoming more fitted] to join in the chorus on high, which, as death successively removes them, is continually increasing by the accession [i.e. addition] of fresh voices.
>
> [Redemption] ... is not an act of mere mercy, but of mercy harmonizing with justice. It is not an act of power only, but of unexampled and expensive love. 'Thou hast redeemed us by thy blood!'
>
> The sentence announced by the law against transgressors was death. And therefore when Messiah became our surety to satisfy the law for us, he must die... His was a bloody death. When he was in great agony in Gethsemane, his 'sweat was as great drops of blood, falling down to the ground'. His blood flowed when he gave his back to smiters, under the painful strokes of the scourging he endured previous to his crucifixion. It flowed from his head when the soldiers, having mocked his character of King, by crowning him with thorns, by their rude blows forced the thorns into his temples. His blood streamed from the wounds made by the spikes, which pierced his hands and feet, when they fastened him to the cross. When he hung upon the cross, his body was full of wounds, and covered

with blood. And, after his death, another large wound was made in his side, from which issued blood and water. Such was the redemption-price he paid for sinners, his blood, the blood of his heart...

This Saviour is very precious to those who believe in him, and who obtain redemption by his blood. How can it be otherwise? Grace like this, when known, must captivate and fix the heart! Not only to save, but to die, and to die for his enemies! Such costly love, productive of such glorious consequences, and to such unworthy creatures!

(*Fifty Sermons on Handel's 'The Messiah'*, Sermon 48)

Praise for redeeming love

*L*et us love, and sing, and wonder,
Let us praise the Saviour's name!
He has hushed the law's loud thunder,
He has quenched Mount Sinai's flame:
He has washed us with his blood,
He has brought us nigh to God.

Let us love the Lord who bought us,
Pitied us when enemies;
Called us by his grace, and taught us,
Gave us ears, and gave us eyes:
He has washed us with his blood,
He presents our souls to God.

Let us sing though fierce temptations
Threaten hard to bear us down!
For the Lord, our strong salvation,
Holds in view the conqueror's crown:
He, who washed us with his blood,
Soon will bring us home to God.

Let us wonder; grace and justice
Join and point to mercy's store;
When through grace in Christ our trust is,
Justice smiles, and asks no more:
He, who washed us with his blood,
Has secured our way to God.

Let us praise, and join the chorus
Of the saints, enthroned on high;
Here they trusted him before us,
Now their praises fill the sky:
'Thou hast washed us with thy blood;
Thou art worthy, Lamb of God!'

Hark! The name of Jesus, sounded
Loud, from golden harps above!
Lord, we blush, and are confounded;
Faint our praises, cold our love!
Wash our souls and songs with blood,
For by thee we come to God.

(Olney Hymns, Book 3, Hymn 82)

S uggested Scripture readings: Revelation 5

'Worthy are you ... for you were slain, and purchased for God with
your blood men from every tribe and tongue and people and nation'
(Rev. 5:9).

To whom shall we go?

When you open your Bible and read of the chronic idolatry of the Israelites it is hard not to feel impatient with them. You would think that sooner or later they would have been convinced that real joy could not be found in the little gilded 'godlets' of this world. But if we are honest with ourselves, we too, though we know better, are tempted to seek happiness where it cannot be found. The following sermon excerpts and hymns warn of the utter foolishness of attempting to find happiness without having God at the epicentre of our lives.

Can the world afford [i.e. provide] a peace which shall abide and cheer the heart under all the changing circumstances incident to us in this mortal state? Can it propose any good, any honours, profit or pleasures, worthy of being compared with the honour which cometh from God only, the light of his countenance, and the riches of glory? Can the influence of the world preserve us from trouble, or support us under it, or deliver us out of it? Has it any charms capable of soothing the anguish of a wounded conscience? Can it obviate the stroke, or overcome the fear, of death? Or can it inspire the soul with confidence and joy, in the contemplation of that approaching day when we must all appear before the tribunal of the supreme Judge? That the world, if we possessed the whole of it, cannot do these things for us is acknowledged by many and felt by all.

I speak first to you who are ... wearied in seeking happiness where it is not to be found... While you are pursuing the wealth or honours of this world, or wasting your time and strength in the indulgence of sensual appetites, and look no higher, are you, indeed, happy and satisfied? ... With what face can you [i.e. how can you dare to] charge the professors of religion [i.e. Christians] with hypocrisy, if you pretend to satisfaction in these ways? We have trodden them far enough ourselves to be assured that there are feelings in your heart which contradict your assertion. You know that you are not happy, and we know it likewise.

(*Fifty Sermons on Handel's 'The Messiah'*, Sermons 31, 14)

Jesus is the light, the life, the sun of the soul that knows him, according to the revelation given in the Scriptures of his person, offices, and grace. And, as the most magnificent palace would be but a dungeon if it had no apertures [i.e. windows] to admit the light, so the whole creation would be dark and dreary to his people, were it possible that they could be excluded from his presence.

(Sermon on 1 Thessalonians 4:16-17 entitled 'The Great Advent')

Will ye also go away?
John 6:67-69

When any turn from Zion's way
(Alas, what numbers do!),
Methinks I hear my Saviour say,
'Wilt thou forsake me too?'

Ah, Lord, with such a heart as mine,
Unless thou hold me fast,
I feel I must, I shall, decline,
And prove like them at last.

Yet thou alone hast power, I know,
To save a wretch like me;
To whom, or whither, could I go,
If I should turn from thee?

Beyond a doubt I rest assured
Thou art the Christ of God;

Who hast eternal life secured
By promise and by blood.

The help of men and angels joined
Could never reach my case;
Nor can I hope relief to find,
But in thy boundless grace.

No voice but thine can give me rest,
And bid my fears depart;
No love but thine can make me blessed,
And satisfy my heart.

What anguish has that question stirred,
If I will also go?
Yet, Lord, relying on thy word,
I humbly answer, 'No!'

(*Olney Hymns*, Book 1, Hymn 115)

None upon earth I desire besides thee

H ow tedious and tasteless the hours,
    When Jesus no longer I see;
Sweet prospects, sweet birds, and sweet flowers
Have lost all their sweetness with me:
The midsummer sun shines but dim,
The fields strive in vain to look gay;
But when I am happy in him,
December's as pleasant as May.

His name yields the richest perfume,
And sweeter than music his voice;
His presence disperses my gloom,
And makes all within me rejoice:
I should, were he always thus nigh,
Have nothing to wish or to fear;

No mortal so happy as I,
My summer would last all the year.

Content with beholding his face,
My all to his pleasure resigned;
No changes of season or place
Would make any change in my mind:
While blessed with a sense of his love,
A palace a toy would appear;
And prisons would palaces prove,
If Jesus would dwell with me there.

Dear Lord, if indeed I am thine,
If thou art my sun and my song;
Say, why do I languish and pine,
And why are my winters so long?
Oh, drive these dark clouds from my sky,
Thy soul-cheering presence restore,
Or take me unto thee on high,
Where winter and clouds are no more!

(*Olney Hymns*, Book 1, Hymn 46)

*S*uggested Scripture reading: John 6:41-71

'*Lord, to whom shall we go? You have words of eternal life*'
(John 6:69).

Amazing grace

On New Year's Day, 1773, at the age of forty-seven, John Newton preached a sermon on I Chronicles 17:16-17. This passage records

King David's words in which he marvels at the goodness of God, who took a humble shepherd boy like himself and made him the mighty king over the Lord's people. David expresses his humility and worship in two simple questions: 'Who am I ... and what is my house?' The passage goes on to record David's sheer amazement at the gracious promises regarding the future of David's dynasty. Below is a transcription of Newton's sermon notes on this passage.

Newton offers much that will help us follow David's example of humble adoration of the goodness of God towards us in the past as well as for what he will yet do for us in the future.

[Introduction]

The Lord bestows many blessings upon his people, but unless he likewise gives them a thankful heart, they lose much of the comfort they might have in them. And this is not only a blessing in itself but an earnest of more. When David was peacefully settled in the kingdom, he purposed to express his gratitude by building a place for the ark. This honour the Lord had appointed for his son Solomon, but he graciously accepted David's intention, for he not only notices the poor services of his people, but even [their] desires to serve him, when they spring from a principle of love, though opportunity should be wanting. He sent him a message by Nathan assuring him that his son should build the house and establish his kingdom. This filled his heart with praise. My text is part of his acknowledgement. Omitting David's personal concerns, I would accommodate them to our own use as a proper subject for our meditations on the entrance of a new year. They lead us to a consideration of past mercies and future hopes and intimate the frame of mind which becomes [i.e. is fitting for] us when we contemplate what the Lord has done for us.

1. The frame of mind: humility and admiration

'Who am I ...?' This question should be always upon our minds. Who am I? What was I when the Lord began to manifest his purposes of love? This was often inculcated upon Israel, 'Thou shalt remember...' Look unto the pit from which we were taken. Lord, what is man?

At that time we were:

Miserable

Shut up under the law and unbelief. What must have been the event had the Lord not left us there? After a few years spent in vanity, we must have sunk to rise no more.

Rebellious

Blinded by the god of this world. We had not so much as a desire of deliverance. Instead of desiring the Lord's help, we breathed a spirit of defiance against him. His mercy came to us not only undeserved but undesired. Yea, few [of] us but resisted [i.e. there were few of us who did not resist] his calls, and when he knocked at the door of our hearts endeavoured to shut him out till he overcame us by the power of his grace. See our proper characteristics (Titus 3:3).

[Undeserving]

It was the Lord against whom we sinned and who showed us mercy. He needed not [do so]. What just cause of admiration that he should appoint such salvation, in such a way, in favour of such helpless, worthless creatures!

2. That thou hast brought me hitherto

Here let us look back.

Before conversion

His providential care preserving us from a thousand seen, [and] millions of unseen, dangers when we knew him not. His secret guidance leading us by a way which we knew not, till his time of love came.

At conversion

The means by which he wrought upon us, supports [us] in the time of conviction, and the never-to-be-forgotten hour when he enabled us to hope in his mercy.

Since we were enabled to give up our names to him

Mercy and goodness have followed us. In temporals [i.e. earthly things], he has led and fed us. Many have fallen when we have been preserved; if afflicted, we have found him a present help in trouble. Some may say, 'With my staff I passed over this Jordan' [see Genesis 32:10]. In spirituals [i.e., spiritual things], preserving us from wasting sins, from gross errors, or restoring and healing, maintaining his hold in our hearts, notwithstanding so much opposition, so many temptations and provocations; the comforts we have had in secret and public worship, the seasonable and un-doubted answers to prayer; grace [shown] to any dear to us, peace in our families, his blessing us with a church and a people.

3. Are these small things?

Yes, compared to what follows — he has spoken for a great while to come, even to eternity. Present mercies are but earn-ests of his love, present comforts but foretastes of the joy to which we are hastening. Oh, that crown, that kingdom, that eternal weight of glory! We are travelling home to God. We shall soon see Jesus and never complain of sin, sorrow, temptation, or desertion any more.

He has dealt with us according to the estate of a man of high degree. He found us upon the dunghill and has made us companions of princes; [he has found us] in a wilderness [and] he has led us to the City of God.

From hence we infer:

Love, gratitude, obedience

Romans 12:1 ['Therefore I urge you, brethren, by the mercies of God, to present your bodies a living and holy sacrifice, acceptable to God, which is your spiritual service of worship'].

Trust and confidence

We have good reason to cast our cares upon him and to be satisfied with his appointments [i.e. with what he has appointed for us]. Hitherto 'he has done all things well' [Mark 7:37].

Patience

Yet a little while and we shall be at home. Romans 13:11 ['... knowing the time, that it is already the hour for you to awaken from sleep; for now salvation is nearer to us than when we believed'].

[Conclusion]

We are spared thus far — but some, I fear, are strangers to the promises. You are entered upon a new year. It may be your last. You are still at present barren trees in the vineyard. Oh, fear lest the sentence should go forth — 'Cut it down'! [Luke 13:7].

(Quoted in Cecil, *John Newton*, p. 365)

Newton also composed a hymn on this same Scripture passage (presumably in conjunction with the sermon) entitled 'Faith's

Review and Expectation'. It too is a model of humble, grateful, personal worship. Today this hymn is known as 'Amazing Grace'. How ironic that God would take a juvenile delinquent, who once composed a song rudely ridiculing the captain of the ship on which he served, and later make him the author of what is arguably the best-known hymn on Planet Earth!

The hymn is quoted below in the form in which it was originally published in the *Olney Hymns*. You will notice that the traditional last verse, 'When we've been there ten thousand years...', is not included, since it was not written by Newton, but was added in 1909 by Edwin Othello Excell, a singer, hymn-writer, and publisher from Chicago.[5]

Faith's review and expectation

A mazing grace! (How sweet the sound!)
That saved a wretch like me!
I once was lost, but now am found,
Was blind, but now I see.

'Twas grace that taught my heart to fear,
And grace my fears relieved;
How precious did that grace appear,
The hour I first believed!

Through many dangers, toils and snares,
 I have already come;
'Tis grace hath brought me safe thus far,
 And grace will lead me home.

The Lord has promised good to me,
His word my hope secures;
He will my shield and portion be,
As long as life endures.

Yes, when this flesh and heart shall fail,
And mortal life shall cease;

I shall possess, within the veil,
A life of joy and peace.

The earth shall soon dissolve like snow,
The sun forbear to shine;
But God, who called me here below
Will be for ever mine.

> (*Olney Hymns,* Book 1, Hymn 41)

S uggested Scripture reading: 1 Chronicles 17:1-27

'Who am I, O LORD God, and what is my house that you have
brought me thus far?' (1 Chr. 17:16).

Family worship

Spiritual leadership of children

Newton began his practice of family worship five or six years into his marriage after reading Philip Doddridge's book *The Rise and Progress of Religion in the Soul*. The impact of Newton's regular spiritual leadership in the home is astounding and encouraging. So powerfully blessed was the family's morning worship that household servants (who were required to attend) came to saving faith in Christ. Eliza Cunningham, an orphaned, twelve-year-old niece, came to live with the Newtons in London. Her uncle's public preaching, coupled with private family worship, made a profound impression on her and she was converted shortly before her death from tuberculosis at the age of fourteen. Young ministers and ministerial students were often found in attendance during morning worship in the Newtons' home, learning from him how to conduct worship not only in the pulpit, but in their homes.

Since few men today have been fortunate enough to have such a mentor in the area of family worship, this letter offering advice on how to conduct family worship will come as welcome advice from a wise, experienced, faithful man like Newton.

A neglect of family prayer is, I am afraid, too common amongst professors [i.e. professing Christians] today. I am glad that you consider it both as a duty and a privilege, and are by grace determined that, when you shall commence

The Old Vicarage, Olney, the home of John and Mary Newton during his
ministry in the town

master of a family, you will worship God with all your house...

I am afraid I shall not answer your expectations ... concerning the most proper method of conducting family worship. The circumstances of families are so various that no determinate rules can be laid down, nor has the Word of God prescribed any; because, being of universal obligation, it is wisely and graciously accommodated to suit the different situations of his people. You must, therefore, as to circumstantials [i.e. practical details], judge for yourself. You will do well to pursue such a method as you shall find most convenient to yourself and family, without scrupulously binding yourself, when the Scripture has left you free.

We have no positive precept enjoining [i.e. requiring of] us any set time for prayer, nor even how often we should pray, either in public or private; though expressions of 'continuing instant in prayer', 'praying without ceasing', and the like, plainly intimate that prayer should be frequent... Indeed a person who lives in the exercise of faith and love, and who finds by experience that it is good for him to draw nigh to God, will not want to be told how often he must pray, any more than how often he must converse with an earthly friend. Those whom we love, we love to be much with... However, I think that family prayer ... [should be] performed at least daily, and, when unavoidable hindrances do not prevent, twice a day. Though all times and seasons are alike to the Lord, and his ear is always open whenever we have a heart to call upon him; yet to *us* there is a peculiar suitableness in beginning and closing the day with prayer... You will, of course, choose those hours when you are least liable to be incommoded [i.e. to be interrupted] by the calls of business, and when the family can assemble with the most convenience ... it is best not to defer evening prayer till late, if it can be well avoided, lest some who join in the exercise, and perhaps the person himself who leads in it, should be too weary or sleepy to give a due attention...

I think, with you, that it is very expedient and proper that reading a portion of the Word of God should be ordinarily a part of our family worship; so likewise to sing a hymn or psalm, or part of one, at discretion; provided there are some persons in the family who have enough of a musical ear and voice to conduct the singing in a tolerable manner; otherwise, perhaps it may be better omitted. If you read and sing, as well as pray, care should be taken that the combined services do not run into an inconvenient length.

The chief thing to be attended to is, that it may be a spiritual service; and the great evil to be dreaded and guarded against in the exercise of every duty that returns frequently upon us is formality... Family prayer ... may come in time to be as mechanically performed [as the striking of a clock] unless we are continually looking to the Lord to keep our hearts alive...

By leading in the worship of God before children ... a man gives bond (as it were) for his behaviour, and adds strength to every other motive which should engage him to abstain from all appearances of evil. It should be a constant check upon our language and tempers in the presence of our families to consider that we began the day, and propose to end it with them, in prayer...

The proper exercise of family prayer ... is a happy means of instructing children ... in the great truths of religion, of softening their prejudices, and inspiring them with a temper [i.e. an attitude] of respect and affection, which will dispose them to cheerful obedience, and make them unwilling to grieve or offend. In this instance, as in every other, we may observe that the Lord's commands to his people are not arbitrary appointments, but that, so far as they are consciously complied with, they have an evident tendency and suitableness to promote our own advantage. He requires us to acknowledge him in our families, for our own sakes; not because he has need of our poor services, but because we have need of his blessing, and without the influence of his grace (which is promised to all who seek it) are sure to be unhappy in ourselves and in all our connections.

(Forty-One Letters on Religious Subjects, Letter 4)

Men, let's follow Newton's lead and not allow another generation of young men to grow up without experiencing the advantage of at least knowing what family worship is supposed to look like! Make it easier for your sons to be faithful in this all-but-abandoned ministry in their future homes by showing them how it is done. Talk to other fathers whom you respect and find out what they are doing with their families (start with your pastor!). Make the hard choice to be different from the world around you. Say 'no' to the uncontrolled busyness that is so common in today's families. Turn off the TV and the computer, spend less time playing sports, open your Bibles and begin to read out loud!

Suggested Scripture readings: Deuteronomy 6:1-9; Psalm 78:1-8

> *'He ... commanded our fathers*
> *That they should teach them to their children,*
> *That the generation to come might know, even the children*
> *yet to be born...'*
> (Ps. 78:5-6).

Children away from home

Just a few months ago, I took my oldest child to begin his freshman year of college and drove home for twelve hours with an indescribable ache in my heart. Life at our house is just not the same without him. While we talk on the phone every day and have had some wonderful spiritual conversations, long-distance parenting is definitely a challenge.

The letters quoted below were written by Newton to his niece, Betsy, whom he raised as a daughter, while she was away at boarding school between the ages of ten and fifteen. The letters contain fairly typical parental advice concerning school and news from home, but they also express Newton's tender love and deep concern for Betsy's spiritual condition. He offers her warm, spiritual counsel concerning her profession of faith and practical advice on prayer and Bible reading.

My dear child, pray to him, and never be content or satisfied till you feel your desire and love fixed upon him. Nothing less will content me for you. If you should behave yourself to me and your mamma with the greatest tenderness, affection, and attention as you grow up (as I hope you will, and you yourself are sensible [i.e. aware that] you ought), still I should weep over you, if I saw you negligent and ungrateful towards the Lord. We love you, and would do much to show it; but we could not, we dare not, be crucified for you. This was such love as he only could show; judge what a return it calls for from you. Not to love the Lord is a disposition the height of wickedness and the depth of misery.

When you read our Saviour's discourses recorded by the evangelists, attend as if you saw him with your own eyes standing before you; and, when you try to pray, assure yourself, before you begin, that he is actually in the room with you, and that his ear is open to every word you say. This will make you serious, and it will likewise encourage you, when you consider that you are not speaking into the air, or to one who is a great way off; but to one who is very near you, to your best Friend, who is both able and willing to give you everything that is good for you.

It is my frequent prayer that you may be wiser than I was at your time of life; that you may have grace to remember your Creator and Redeemer while you are yet young. Depend upon it, my dear, whenever you really know the Lord, you will be sorry you did not know him sooner; whenever you experience that pleasure which is only to be found in loving and serving him, you will wish you had loved and served him (if possible) from your very cradle.

Your conscience tells you that you are a great sinner, and that makes you afraid; but, when the Lord gives you faith, you will see and understand that the blood of Jesus Christ cleanses from all sin; then you will love him; and when you love him, you will find it easy and pleasant to serve him; and then you will long to see him who died for you — and, as it is impossible to see him in this world, you will be glad that you are not to stay here always; you will be willing to die, that you may be with him where he is. In the meantime, I hope you will pray to him, and wait for his time to reveal himself to you, endeavouring to avoid whatever you know to be wrong and displeasing to him, and sometimes, I hope, you will feel your heart soft and tender, and serious thoughts and desires rising in your mind; when you do, then think, 'Now is the Lord calling me!' And say, as Samuel did, 'Speak, Lord, for thy servant heareth.' He does not call with an audible voice, but he speaks to the heart in a way not to be described by words. When we are grieved and ashamed for our sins; when we are affected with what we read and hear of him, of his love, his sufferings, and his death; when we see and feel that nothing but his favour can make us happy — then we may be sure the Lord is near.

Sometimes, when I consider what a world you are growing up into, and what snares and dangers young people are exposed to, with little experience to help them, I have some painful feelings for you. The other day I was at Deptford, and saw a ship launched: she slipped easily into the water; the people on board shouted; the ship looked clean and gay [i.e. bright], she was fresh painted, and her colours flying. But I looked at her with a sort of pity: 'Poor ship,' I thought, 'you are now in port and in safety; but ere long you must go to sea. Who can tell what storms you may meet with hereafter, and to what hazards you may be exposed; how weather-beaten you may be before you return to port again, or whether you may return at all!' Then my thoughts turned from the ship to my child. It seemed an emblem of your present state: you are now, as it were, in a safe harbour; but by and by you must launch out into the world, which may well be compared to a tempestuous sea. I could even now almost weep at the resemblance; but I take courage; my hopes are greater than my fears. I know there is an infallible Pilot, who has the winds and the waves at his command. There is hardly a day passes in which I do not entreat him to take charge of you. Under his care I know you will be safe; he can guide you, unhurt, amidst the storms, and rocks, and dangers, by which you might otherwise suffer, and bring you, at last, to the haven of eternal rest. I hope you will seek him while you are young, and I am sure he will be the friend of them that seek him sincerely; then you will be happy, and I shall rejoice. Nothing will satisfy me but this; though I should live to see you settled to the greatest advantage in temporal matters, except you love him, and live in his fear and favour, you would appear to me quite miserable. I think it would go near to break my heart, for next to your dear mamma, there is nothing so dear to me in this world as you. But the Lord gave you to me, and I have given you to him again, many and many a time on my knees, and therefore I hope you must, and will, and shall be his.

You are growing up in a world which is full of sins, snares, troubles, and dangers. Will you not cry to him then, 'My Father, thou art the Guide of my youth?' You have encouragement to seek him, for he himself both invites and commands you to do it; and if obligations and gratitude can prevail, there is no friend like him, whose mercies are new every morning, and who died upon the cross to redeem us from misery.

I can remember getting into corners by myself, and praying with some earnestness, before I was eight years old. Afterwards, alas, I proved rebellious, I cast off his fear, and would have my own way; and thereby I plunged myself into an abundance of sin and misery. But I hope you will be more obedient. Think of him as often as you can; make a point of praying to him in secret, remembering that when you are most alone, he is still with you. When you pray, endeavour simply to express your wants and feelings just as if you were speaking to me. Fine words and phrases some people abound in; but true prayer is the genuine language of the heart, which the Lord understands and accepts, however brokenly expressed.

(*Letters intended as a sequel to Cardiphonia*, 'Twenty-one Letters to Miss ...', Letters 1, 4, 5, 9, 12, 18, 20).

S uggested Scripture readings: Genesis 18:17-19; Ephesians 6:1-4; Colossians 3:20-21

'I have no greater joy than this, to hear of my children walking in the truth' (3 John 4).

Spiritual leadership of wives

As a merchant sailor by vocation, Newton's first few years of marriage to Mary required the couple to endure many months of lonely separation. They kept up their relationship, as best they could, by faithfully writing letters — letters which must have seemed to take an eternity to cross the vast Atlantic Ocean. At one point, a group of Mary's letters were accidentally forwarded to the wrong destination and missed John altogether. Not having heard from his wife for so many months, Newton wrongly came to the conclusion that she must be dead. During that time, he wondered if his own failure to take the initiative in spiritual matters in their marriage had caused God to remove her from his life.

I was ... greatly hindered by a cowardly, reserved spirit; I was afraid of being thought precise [i.e. narrow-minded]; and, though I could not live without prayer, I durst [i.e. dared] not propose it even to my wife, till she herself first put me upon it [i.e. suggested it to me]; so far was I from those expressions of zeal and love which seemed so suitable to the case of one who has had much forgiven...

I thought my unfaithfulness to God had deprived me of her, especially my backwardness in speaking of spiritual things, which I could hardly attempt even to her.

(*An Authentic Narrative*, Letter 12)

In contrast to his early failures, the following extract gives practical advice on a husband's spiritual leadership and fellowship with his wife. He mentions the importance of husbands and wives praying regularly together, specifically advising men not to make the mistake of failing to encourage their wives to pray as well.

When husband and wife are happily partakers of the same faith, it seems expedient, and for their mutual good, that, besides their private devotions, and joining in family prayer, they should pray together. They have many wants, mercies, and concerns, in common with each other, and

distinct from the rest of the family. The manner in which
they should improve [i.e. spend] a little time in this joint
exercise cannot well be prescribed by a third person: yet I
will venture to suggest one thing; and the rather, as I do not
remember to have met with it in print. I conceive that it may
prove much to their comfort to pray alternately, not only
the husband with and for the wife, but the wife with and for
the husband. The Spirit of God, by the apostle, has expressly restrained women from the exercise of spiritual gifts
in public; but I apprehend the practice I am speaking of can
no way interfere with that restriction. I suppose them in
private together, and then I judge it to be equally right and
proper for either of them to pray with the other. If you ask,
how often they should pray together, I think the oftener the
better, provided it does not break in upon their duties; once
a day at least; and if there is a choice of hours, it might be as
well at some distance from their other seasons of worship.
But I would observe, as before, that in matters not expressly
commanded, prudence and experience must direct.

I have written upon a supposition that you use extempore prayer [i.e. as opposed to written prayers]; but as there
are many heads of families who fear the Lord, and have not
yet attained liberty to pray extempore before others, I
would add that their inability in this respect, whether real,
or whether only proceeding from fear, and an undue regard
to self, will not justify them in the omission of family
prayer. Helps [i.e. devotional books] may be procured... If
they begin with a form [i.e. a set prayer], not with a design
to confine themselves always to one, but make it a part of
their secret pleading at the throne of grace that they may be
favoured with the gift and sprit of prayer, and [if they] ac-
custom themselves, while they use a form, to intersperse
some petitions of their own; there is little doubt but they
will in time find a growth in liberty and ability, and at
length lay their book entirely aside. For it being every

believer's duty to worship God in his family, his promise may be depended upon to give them a sufficiency in all things, for those services which he requires of them.

Happy is the family where the worship of God is constantly and conscientiously maintained. Such houses are temples, in which the Lord dwells, and castles garrisoned by a divine power. I do not say that, by honouring God in your house, you will wholly escape a share in the trials incident to the present uncertain state of things. A measure of such trials will be necessary for the exercise and manifestation of your graces, to give you a more convincing proof of the truth and sweetness of the promises made to a time of affliction, to mortify the body of sin, and to wean you more effectually from the world. But this I will confidently say, that the Lord will both honour and comfort those who thus honour him. Seasons will occur in which you shall know, and probably your neighbours shall be constrained to take notice, that he has not bid you seek him in vain. If you meet with troubles, they shall be accompanied by supports, and followed by deliverance; and you shall upon many occasions experience that he is your protector, preserving you and yours from the evils by which you will see others suffering around you.

(Forty-One Letters on Religious Subjects, Letter 4)

Husbands, spiritual passivity has devastating effects not only for your children, but also for your wife. In the early years of my marriage, I confess to my shame that I hardly ever prayed with my wife. I experienced tremendous guilt knowing what the Lord expected of me as a husband. Eventually, I repented of my failure to take the spiritual initiative in my marriage. As I sought my wife's forgiveness, she told me that she had been assuming that the reason that I didn't pray with her was the result of some flaw or weakness in her. I assured her that this was not the case, and that I was fully responsible for my spiritual lack of leadership. I was devastated and grieved to see that simply by 'doing nothing' in the spiritual arena, I had been causing my wife deep sorrow. Men, I strongly urge you to avoid this common, yet grievous sin. As Newton says, 'fear ... or an undue regard for self will not justify' us before God for failing to exercise spiritual leadership of our wives.

Suggested **Scripture readings**: Ephesians 5:25-33; Colossians 3:18-19; 1 Peter 3:1-7

'You husbands ... live with your wives in an understanding way, as with someone weaker, since she is a woman; and show her honour as a fellow heir of the grace of life, so that your prayers will not be hindered' (I Peter 3:7).

Evangelism

Ambassadors for Christ

When it comes to opening our mouths and talking to unconverted friends and loved ones about our love for the Lord Jesus, most of us are somewhat timid and fearful. The thought of being overtly rejected, or of being unable to answer a thorny theological or ethical question, is unnerving. My wife and I have lived in the same house for almost twenty years and I am ashamed to say that we have not been very faithful or zealous in our outreach to our neighbours. I could give you the same list of reasons that I have offered myself over the years, but since Scripture calls on each of us to 'proclaim the excellencies of him who has called [us] out of darkness into his marvellous light' (1 Peter 2:9), I am ultimately without excuse. We have recently renewed our determination to build relationships with our neighbours for the purpose of telling them about what the Lord has done in our lives. The sermon excerpt and the hymn that follow are just the sort of encouragement and rebuke that we both need in order to make good our new commitment to reach out.

Newton lived in an age in which he saw encouraging changes in regard to evangelistic preaching and ministry. In a letter written when he was seventy years of age, he rejoiced that:

> The times are dark; but perhaps they were darker in England sixty years ago, when … people were perishing for lack of knowledge… Every year the gospel is planted in new

places — ministers are still raising up — the work is still spreading. I am not sure [whether] in the year 1740, there was a single parochial minister [i.e. minister of a parish in the Church of England] who was publicly known as a gospel preacher in the whole kingdom: now we have I know not how many, but I think not fewer than four hundred.

(Quoted in Hindmarsh, *John Newton and the Evangelical Tradition*, p. 327)

The sermon quoted below was delivered by Newton, in his own pulpit in London, to a congregation made up of ministers who were members of the Society for Promoting Religious Knowledge among the Poor. In his opening comments, he mentions that this was the largest gathering of ministerial colleagues that he had ever addressed in his twenty-three years of ministry. The text for his sermon was Proverbs 11:30, which says, 'He who is wise wins souls.' In this message, Newton reminded his fellow ministers (and us today) that our role in evangelism is that of a reliable herald or ambassador delivering a message on behalf of the one who sent us. We should not embellish the gospel message entrusted to us, nor should we be unduly concerned about the manner in which those to whom we speak receive us. There is a real relief that comes from knowing that all that God requires of his messengers is faithfulness to deliver the message entrusted to us.

What should we think of a statesman who, having formed a wise and noble plan for the benefit of a kingdom, and having the means necessary to accomplish it within his power, should be deterred from carrying it into execution, though it was approved by all the competent judges, merely because he could not bear to be misunderstood or misrepresented by the very lowest of the people, or by the children who play in the street? His want of spirit upon such a supposition would, doubtless, be esteemed a want of wisdom. But this is a faint representation of our folly if, believing ourselves to be the servants of God, being convinced, as we say, of the worth and danger of souls, and knowing that the gospel of God committed to our trust (1 Thessalonians 2:4) is the only possible means of their recovery, a regard to the fear or favour of men should prevail on us to suppress or soften our message, and to accommodate ourselves to their taste, instead of conforming to our instructions, lest we should displease them. Would an earthly king bear with an ambassador who was guilty of such treachery?

We cannot, my brethren, think too humbly of ourselves; but we may magnify our office, and we ought. In this sense, at least, 'we are ambassadors for Christ', that the message we are to deliver is not ours, but his, by whom we are sent. We are not answerable for the success, but we are under the strongest obligation to be faithful. And he, whose we are, and whom we serve, is well able to support us. Let us not fear the reproach of men, nor be afraid of their revilings [i.e. the abuse they may shower upon us]... Jesus endured the cross, and despised the shame for them and for us; he was buffeted, spit on, treated as a madman, a demoniac, and laughed to scorn. Let us go forth, bearing his reproach, in meekness of wisdom instructing those who oppose, not rendering railing [i.e. insult] for railing, but pitying and praying for them; but let us be firm and unmoved, and not hesitate to speak the truth in love, whether they will hear or whether they will forbear. We shall not speak wholly in vain; and to be instrumental in saving one soul from death is an honour sufficient to compensate for all the slights and contempts we can meet with from an unkind world...

He who is wise to win souls loves his fellow-creatures; but he cannot fear them, because he fears the Lord. He will neither provoke nor dread their frowns, nor will he meanly [i.e. obsequiously] court their smiles. He knows that if they receive his message, they will love him for the truth's sake, and he neither expects nor desires their favour upon other terms. By the cross of Christ he is crucified to the world, and the world to him (Galatians 6:14). He has chosen his side

(Joshua 24:15). He will serve the Lord, and he will use his utmost influence to prevail on others to serve him likewise; so far as he succeeds, he feels a joy superior to the joy of harvest, or of those who divide the spoil (Isaiah 9:3).

('The Best Wisdom', a sermon preached at St Mary Woolnoth)

The hymn quoted below picks up on the theme of this sermon, addressing us as ambassadors for Christ.

We are ambassadors for Christ
2 Corinthians 5:20

*T*hy message, by the preacher, seal,
    And let thy power be known;
That every sinner here may feel
The word is not his own.

Amongst the foremost of the throng
Who dare thee to thy face,
He in rebellion stood too long,
And fought against thy grace.

But grace prevailed, he mercy found,
And now by thee is sent,
To tell his fellow-rebels round,
And call them to repent.

In Jesus, God is reconciled,
The worst may be forgiven;
Come, and he'll own you as a child,
And make you heirs of heaven.

Oh, may the word of gospel truth
Your chief desires engage;

And Jesus be your guide in youth,
Your joy in hoary age.

Perhaps the year that's now begun
May prove to some their last;
The sands of life may soon be run,
The day of grace be past.

Think, if you slight this embassy,
And will not warning take,
When Jesus in the clouds you see,
What answer will you make?

(Olney Hymns, Book 2, Hymn 27)

S uggested Scripture readings: Proverbs 11:30; Mark
4:26-32; 2 Corinthians 5:14-21; 2 Timothy 4:1-5

> *'Therefore, we are ambassadors for Christ, as though God were
> making an appeal through us; we beg you on behalf of Christ, be
> reconciled to God' (2 Cor. 5:20).*

Christ, the great divider

In these pluralistic days of politically correct 'tolerance', it isn't hard
to get someone to agree with you that there is a God. In my experience at least, scepticism about the existence of God has to a large
extent faded; in fact, denying the existence of the supernatural is
regarded by many as very unsophisticated, and being a complete
atheist is going out of fashion. However, when it comes to the
person and work of Jesus Christ it is another matter. If you bring up
the name of Jesus Christ in a conversation, the polite smiles which
greeted the subject of God will often quickly give way to scowls of
offence at your shockingly narrow views. The exclusivity of the

person and work of Christ was in Newton's day, and is in our own, the great divider among world religions — and between neighbours.

The excerpts that follow remind us that the doctrine of the deity of Christ is not a peripheral issue. Newton's evangelistic preaching insists that what a man thinks about Jesus Christ determines his eternal destiny. He spoke boldly, not just about God the Father, but about God the Son as he became flesh and dwelt among us. Newton asked men and women the same fundamental question that Jesus asks the Pharisees: 'What do you think about the Christ, whose son is he?'

> This doctrine [i.e. the deity of Christ] is, in my view, the great foundation stone upon which all true religion is built; but, alas! in the present day, it is the stumbling block of offence, upon which too many, fondly presuming upon their own wisdom, fall and are broken. I am so far from wondering that any should doubt of it that I am firmly persuaded none can truly believe it, however plainly set forth in Scripture, unless it be revealed to them from heaven; or in the apostle's words, that 'no one can call Jesus Christ Lord but by the Holy Ghost' [1 Corinthians 12:3]... I know nothing that can obviate the objections the reasoning mind is ready to form against it, but a real conviction of the sinfulness of sin... Then the necessity of a Redeemer, and the necessity of this Redeemer's being almighty, is seen and felt, with an evidence which bears down on all opposition; for neither the efficacy of his atonement and intercession, nor his sufficiency to guide, save, protect, and feed those who trust in him, can be conceived of without it.
>
> (*Cardiphonia*, 'Seven Letters to Mrs —,' Letter 2)

> Many of the heathens believed that God reigned. [But] the Christian doctrine is, that the Lord God omnipotent exerciseth his dominion and government in the person of Christ. 'The Father loveth the Son, and hath committed all things into his hand' [John 3:35]. And thus our Lord, after

his resurrection, assured his disciples, 'All power is committed unto me in heaven and in earth' [Matthew 28:18].

(*Fifty Sermons on Handel's 'The Messiah,'* Sermon 36)

This doctrine [of the deity of Christ] is the pillar and
ground of truth. They who have a right sense of the guilt
and power of sin, of the holiness and majesty of God, and of
the host of enemies combined against their peace, must sink
into despair, unless supported by the knowledge of an almighty, omnipresent Saviour... Whatever they thought of
him before, when they know themselves, they cannot entrust their souls to the power or care or compassion of a
creature; and therefore, [they] rejoice that they are warranted and encouraged to commend themselves to him, as
to a faithful Creator.

(Sermon entitled 'The Best Wisdom')

Assure yourselves that there is nothing vain or useless in
the Word of God. Compare one place with another: the Law
with the Gospel, the Prophets with the Evangelists [i.e. the
Gospels]; pray unto God that he would open your understandings to understand the Scriptures, as he did for the
disciples (Luke 24); and in a little time you will find that
Christ is not only spoken of in a few verses, here and there,
but that, as I said before, he is the main scope of every book,
and almost every chapter.

(*Six Discourses as Intended for the Pulpit,* Sermon 5)

I shall content myself with observing this general proof
of the divinity of Christ, that the Scriptures, which were
given to make us wise to salvation, do ascribe to him the
names of God, particularly Jehovah; the essential attributes
of God, such as eternity, omnipresence, omnipotence; the
peculiar works of God [i.e. the works that only God can do],
as creation, providence, redemption, and forgiveness of sin;

and, finally, command us to pay him those divine honours, and to rely on him with that absolute dependence which would be idolatry if referred anywhere below the Supreme Majesty of heaven and earth.

(Sermon entitled, 'On the Saviour, and his Salvation')

What think you of Christ?
Matthew 22:42

'What think you of Christ?' is the test
　　To try both your state and your scheme;
You cannot be right in the rest
　Until you think rightly of him.
As Jesus appears in your view,
As he is beloved or not,
So God is disposéd to you,
And mercy or wrath are your lot.

Some take him a creature to be,
A man, or an angel at most;
Sure, these have not feelings like me,
Nor know themselves wretched and lost:
So guilty, so helpless am I,
I durst [i.e. dare] not confide in his blood,
Nor on his protection rely,
Unless I am sure he is God.

Some call him a Saviour, in word,
But mix their own works with his plan;
And hope he his help will afford,
When they have done all that they can:
If doings prove rather too light
(A little, they own, they may fail),
They purpose to make up full weight
By casting his name in the scale.

Some style [i.e. call] him the pearl of great price,
And say he's the fountain of joys,
Yet feed upon folly and vice,
And cleave to the world and its toys;
Like Judas, the Saviour they kiss,
And, while they salute him, betray;
Ah! What will profession like this
Avail in his terrible day?

If asked, what of Jesus I think,
Though still my best thoughts are but poor;
I say, he's my meat and my drink,
My life, and my strength, and my store;
My Shepherd, my Husband, my Friend,
My Saviour from sin and from thrall [i.e. bondage];
My hope from beginning to end,
My portion, my Lord, and my all.

(Olney Hymns, Book 1, Hymn 89)

Suggested **Scripture readings:** Matthew 22:41-46, John 1:1-18, Colossians 1:15-23

> *'What do you think about the Christ, whose son is he?'*
> (Matt. 22:42).

The cure for unbelief

Newton humbly said of his ministry in London, 'My connections have enlarged — my little name is spread.' They had indeed enlarged! Two years before his ministry in London began, he already had a dozen books published and his writing ministry had spread beyond England to Ireland, Scotland, America and even the continent of Europe, where some of his works were translated into German and Low Dutch.[6]

Commenting on his appointment to the church of St Mary Woolnoth in London, Newton expressed his amazement to his friend Richard Cecil:

> That one of the most ignorant, and most miserable, and those most abandoned of slaves, should be plucked from his forlorn state of exile on the west coast of Africa, and at length be appointed minister of the parish of the first magistrate of the first city in the world — that he should go there, not only to testify of such grace, but stand up as such a singular instance of it — that he should be enabled to record his history, preaching, and writings to the world at large — is a fact I can contemplate with admiration, but never sufficiently estimate.
>
> (Quoted by Cecil, *John Newton*, p.150)

Newton's ever-widening ministry included the publication of several gospel tracts. Below is an excerpt from one entitled *A Dialogue*. It contains an imaginary conversation between a Christian and a friend who, while under great conviction of sin, has not yet placed his faith in Jesus as the only hope of forgiveness. The friend is encouraged to contemplate the absolute sufficiency of Christ's work upon the cross as the cure for such unbelief. Newton's evangelistic ministry was characterized by joyful proclamation to all those who feared that their sins might be too great to be forgiven, or who wondered if they really knew how to believe, that they need look no further than the cross!

> A [Jesus] is now withdrawn from the earth; yet he still says of old, 'Come unto me.' He does not mean that we should climb the clouds, but come to meet him in the ways [that he has appointed].
>
> B Which are they?
>
> A Chiefly these: his Word, his mercy seat [i.e. prayer], and his assemblies [i.e. gatherings of God's people for

worship and preaching]; he converses with his people in his Word; he draws near to them in prayer...

B True, he meets *his people*, but not *me*. I have sought him in these ways many times. I sought him but I found him not. I am weary and ready to faint. I think I shall give all up. He will not look upon me at all — so far from it that [it] is never worse with me than sometimes when I am seeking him in the manner you speak of... If I was sure that he would come at last, I should be willing to wait, but I am afraid he will never meet me, never accept me, no never... What would you have me to do?

A Believe.

B Lord, increase my faith.

A It is a good prayer, and where it expresses the desire of the heart, it is never used in vain.

B But what are the best means?

A The cross of Christ.

B Pray explain yourself.

A Suppose that, knowing all you know at present, the evil of your sin, your own guilt and misery, and suppose that there was no Saviour but Jesus — I say, suppose that, knowing all this, you had lived at the time when he conversed with men in the form of a servant, and, being in a dull and desponding frame, as you are now, you had come, without any apprehensions of what was transacting, to Mount Calvary, just time enough to see Jesus nailed to the cross, and to see him raised on high, the mark [i.e. object] of contempt and cruelty, covered with blood and full of wounds. And suppose [that] while you beheld him thus dying a thousand deaths, as one for the sins of his very murderers, you heard the prayer for them, and his gracious answer to the dying thief. Would not such a sight and such words have sweetly suited the state of your mind? If I mistake not, you think you should almost have interrupted the solemn scene, you would have been ready to run up to him, and say, 'Lord pray *for me too*, remember *me likewise*, when thou art in the kingdom.'

B Indeed, you have read my heart.

A I dare say you are as firmly persuaded in your mind that these things did once happen as if you had been present and seen them with your own eyes.

B I have not the least doubt concerning them.

A Well then, here is the cure for unbelief. Look unto the divine Saviour, as becoming obedient unto death, even the death of the cross for sinners, yea — glorious truth — for the chief of sinners. He loved them and gave himself for them. And why? That they might believe on him as their perfect and eternal Saviour, and love him as their Lord and their God, and be happy. Look upon him in this light, and his promised rest shall be yours. View him as living and dying that he might be able to save to the uttermost, and that whosoever cometh to him might in no wise [i.e. way] be cast out, and then you will find the matter of comfort to your afflicted conscience. This sight rightly applied is the source of your peace, and the fountain of joy. Thus have I explained to you how the cross of Christ is the best means.

B Oh that I could but look up to him, and be saved! Still something hinders me. My natural wretchedness and my spiritual weakness fill me with fears.

A Be not discouraged by the one, nor despair for the other. Jesus is the antidote against the former. His Spirit is the cure of the latter. It is his office to glorify Jesus by taking the things that are his, and showing them to his people, whereby they see the infinite dignity of his person, and the infinite sufficiency of his undertaking, and have faith to receive and apply Jesus to their souls for salvation. It is this good Spirit who fills their minds with joy and peace in believing, and produces all the fruits of righteousness in their lives. May he witness with your spirit that you are a child of God, a member of Christ, and an heir of glory. So shall you possess present peace, and receive future happiness. To the love of the Lord God I commend you. Remember once more, that Jesus died for sinners.

B And I hope he will not cast me out, though I come as a great sinner to him.

A You have his word that he will not, his word that cannot be broken.

B To that then will I trust, the Lord being my helper. 'I come unto thee, Lord Jesus, because thou hast promised not to cast me out, and on thee will wait. Let it be done unto me according to thy word. Amen.'

(Quoted by Cecil, John Newton, Appendix 5)

Suggested **Scripture readings:** John 19:17-42; Colossians 2:13-14; 1 Peter 2:24-25

'He is able ... to save for ever those who draw near to God through him' (Heb. 7:25).

Knowing the will of God

Divine guidance

It Newton's day it was common for people who desired to know God's will regarding some matter to participate in a practice called 'dipping', in which they would take a Bible, open it at random, read the first verse that their eye fell on, and then presume that verse to be infallible guidance from God. As a pastor, I can testify that practices like 'dipping' did not end with the eighteenth century! Over the years, I have been grieved to observe people use Scripture to justify any number of selfish desires and sinful choices, many of which have ended in utter spiritual disaster.

In the letter quoted below on guidance, Newton warns his reader to avoid misusing Scripture, relying on subjective impressions and trusting in 'freedom' in prayer or in dreams when trying to discern God's will. Instead, he suggests that the best way to know the will of God on any matter is to possess 'an habitual frame', or a constant mindset, 'of spiritual wisdom', which comes from a deep knowledge of the Scriptures.

Answer to the question, 'In what manner are we to expect the Lord's promised guidance to influence our judgements, and direct our steps in the path of duty?'

It is well for those who are duly sensible of their own weakness and fallibility, and of the difficulties with which they are surrounded in life, that the Lord has promised to guide his people with his eye, and to cause them to hear a word behind them, saying, 'This is the way, walk ye in it,' when they are in danger of turning aside either to the right hand or to the left. For this purpose, he has given us the written word to be a lamp to our feet, and encouraged us to pray for the teaching of his Holy Spirit, that we may rightly understand and apply it. It is, however, too often seen that many widely deviate from the path of duty, and commit gross and perplexing mistakes, while they profess a sincere desire to know the will of God, and think they have his warrant and authority. This must certainly be owing to misapplication of the rule by which they judge, since the rule itself is infallible, and the promise sure. The Scripture cannot deceive us, if rightly understood; but it may, if perverted, prove the occasion of confirming us in a mistake. The Holy Spirit cannot mislead those who are under his influence; but we may suppose that we are so when we are not. It may not be unseasonable to offer a few thoughts upon a subject of great importance to the peace of our minds, and to the honour of our holy profession.

Many have been deceived as to what they ought to do, or in forming a judgement beforehand of events in which they are nearly concerned, by expecting direction in ways which the Lord has not warranted. I shall mention some of the principal of these, for it is not easy to enumerate them all...

[Some people], when in doubt, have opened the Bible at a venture, and expected to find something to direct them in the first verse they should cast their eye upon. It is no small discredit to this practice that the heathens, who knew not the Bible, used some of their favourite books in the same way ... for if people will be governed by the occurrence of a single text of Scripture, without regarding the context, or duly comparing it with the general tenor of the Word of God, and with their own circumstances, they may commit the greatest extravagances, expect the greatest impossibilities, and contradict the plainest dictates of common sense, while they think they have the Word of God on their side. Can the opening upon [i.e. opening the Bible at] 2 Samuel 7:3, when Nathan said unto David, 'Do all that is in thine heart, for the Lord is with thee,' be sufficient to determine the lawfulness or expediency of actions? Or can a glance of the eye upon our Lord's words to the woman of Canaan (Matthew 15:28), 'Be it unto thee even as thou wilt,' amount to a proof that the present earnest desire of the mind (whatever it may be) shall be surely accomplished? Yet it is certain that matters big with important consequences have been engaged in, and the most sanguine expectations formed, upon no better warrant than dipping (as it is called) upon a text of Scripture.

A sudden strong impression of a text, that seems to have some resemblance to the concern, upon the mind has been accepted by many as an infallible token that they were right, and that things would go just as they would have them: or, on the other hand, if the passage bore a threatening aspect, it has filled them with fears and disquietudes [i.e. anxieties] which they have afterwards found were groundless and unnecessary. These impressions ... have frequently proved no less delusive [than the practice of dipping]. It is allowed that such impressions of a precept or a promise as humble, animate or comfort the soul by giving it a lively [i.e. vivid] sense of the truth contained in the words are profitable and pleasant; and many of the Lord's people have been instructed and supported (especially in a time of trouble) by some seasonable word of grace applied and sealed by his Spirit with power to their hearts. But if impressions or impulses are received as a voice from heaven, directing to such particular actions as could not be proved to be duties without them, a person may be unwarily misled into great evils and gross delusions; and many have been so. There is no doubt but the enemy of our souls, if permitted, can furnish us with Scriptures in abundance in this way, and for these purposes.

Some persons judge of the nature and event of their designs [i.e. the outcome of their plans] by the freedom which they find in prayer. They say they commit their ways to God, seek his direction, and are favoured with much enlargement of spirit; and therefore they cannot doubt but what they have in view is acceptable in the Lord's sight. I would not absolutely reject every plea of this kind, yet without other corroborating evidence, I could not admit it in proof of what it is brought for. It is not *always* easy to determine when we have spiritual freedom in prayer. Self is deceitful; and when our hearts are much fixed and bent upon a thing, this may put words and earnestness into our mouths. Too often we first secretly determine for ourselves, and then come to ask counsel of God; in such a disposition we are ready to catch at everything that may seem to favour our darling scheme; and the Lord, for the detection and chastisement of our hypocrisy (for hypocrisy it is, though perhaps hardly perceptible to ourselves), may answer us according to our idols (see Ezekiel 14:3-4)...

Once more, a remarkable dream has sometimes been thought as decisive as any of the foregoing methods of knowing the will of God. That many wholesome and seasonable admonitions have been received in dreams, I willingly allow; but, though they may be occasionally noticed, to pay a great attention to dreams, especially to be guided by them, to form our sentiments, conduct, or expectations upon them, is superstitious and dangerous. The promises are not made to those who dream, but to those who watch.

Upon the whole, though the Lord may give to some persons, upon some occasions, a hint or encouragement out of the common way, yet expressly to look for and seek his direction in such things as I have mentioned is unscriptural and ensnaring... I have seen some presuming they were doing God service, while acting in contradiction to his express commands. I have known others infatuated to believe a lie, declaring themselves assured, beyond the shadow of a doubt, of things which, after all, never came to pass; and when at length disappointed, Satan has improved [i.e. taken advantage of] the occasion to make them doubt of the plainest and most important truths, and to account their whole former experience a delusion. By these things weak believers have been stumbled, cavils [i.e. objections] and offences against the gospel multiplied, and the ways of truth evil spoken of.

But how then may the Lord's guidance be expected? After what has been premised negatively, the question may be answered in a few words. In general, he guides and directs his people by affording them, in answer to prayer, the light of his Holy Spirit, which enables them to understand and to love the Scriptures. The Word of God is not to be used as a lottery; nor is it designed to instruct us by shreds and scraps, which, detached from their proper places, have no determinate import; but it is to furnish us with just principles, right apprehensions to regulate our judgements and affections, and thereby to influence and direct our conduct. They who study the Scriptures in an humble dependence upon divine teaching are convinced of their own weakness, are taught to make a true estimate of everything around them, are gradually formed into a spirit of submission to the will of God, discover the nature and duties of their several situations and relations in life, and the snares and temptations to which they are exposed. The Word of God dwells richly in them, is a preservative from error, a light to their feet, and a spring of strength and consolation. By treasuring up the doctrines, precepts, promises, examples, and exhortations of Scripture in their minds, and daily comparing themselves with the rule by which they walk, they grow into an habitual frame of spiritual wisdom, and acquire a gracious taste, which enables them to judge of right and wrong with a degree of readiness and certainty, as a musical ear judges of sounds. And they are seldom mistaken, because they are influenced by the love of Christ, which rules in their hearts, and a regard to the glory of God, which is the great object they have in view.

In particular cases, the Lord opens and shuts for them, breaks down walls of difficulty which obstruct their path, or hedges up their way with thorns, when they are in danger of going wrong, by the dispensations of his providence [i.e. by his providential ordering of their circumstances]. They know that their concernments [i.e. concerns] are in his hands; they are willing to follow whither and when he leads; but are afraid of going before him. Therefore they are not impatient: because they believe, they will not make haste, but wait daily upon him in prayer; especially when they find their hearts most engaged in any purpose or pursuit, they are most jealous of being deceived by appearances, and dare not move farther or faster than they can perceive his light shining upon their paths. I express at least their desire, if not their attainment: thus they would be. And though there are seasons when faith languishes, and self too much prevails, this is their general disposition; and the Lord, whom they serve, does not disappoint their expectations. He leads them by a right way, preserves them from a thousand snares, and satisfies them that he is and will be their guide even unto death.

(*Forty-One Letters on Religious Subjects,* Letter 28)

S**uggested Scripture readings:** Proverbs 2:20-22; 3:13-20; 8:1-11

'For you are my rock and my fortress; for your name's sake you will lead me and guide me' (Ps. 31:3).

4.

PASTORAL MINISTRY

What contradictions meet
In ministers' employ!
It is a bitter sweet,
A sorrow full of joy:
No other post affords a place
For equal honour, or disgrace!

Extract from a letter to Mary including an early draft of the hymn 'What contradictions meet in ministers' employ'

The minister and his work

A pastor's joys and griefs

As a pastor myself, it is temping to suppose that the pace of pastoral ministry, along with its inherent private pressures, might have been less demanding in Newton's day. My naive imaginings about ministry in tranquil Buckinghamshire in the eighteenth century could lead to a twinge of jealousy when compared to my frenetic twenty-first-century lifestyle. But a closer examination of Newton's weekly pastoral responsibilities proves that the demands on his time were even greater than my own. Yet, somehow, he managed to get it all done without a computer, a secretary, or a mobile phone!

The eighteenth century was an age in which 'absentee clergymen' were the norm. Newton's hands-on approach to pastoral ministry was a radical departure from what those in his parishes would have come to expect. His sincere desire to serve the people of Olney, many of whom were poor and illiterate, was demonstrated by his frequent visits to their homes, as well as by the regular hospitality practised in the vicarage, which one person described as 'an asylum for the perplexed or afflicted'.[1] Newton's unpretentious nature was evident as he strolled the streets of Olney wearing his rough old seaman's jacket, rather than the traditional clerical garb.

Newton had a deep longing that the gospel should transform the lives of the people under his care. His equally strong desire for their spiritual growth was obvious not only in his pulpit ministry, but also in his labours outside the pulpit. He organized multiple weekly prayer meetings, gatherings for children and times of teaching for the encouragement of both new and mature believers. But perhaps there is no greater evidence of Newton's affection for, and determination to reach into, the hearts and homes of the people of Olney than his faithful labour in writing the hymns which he considered his 'sermons in verse'.

The Lord blessed the efforts of this faithful shepherd. For several years in Olney, there was seldom a week that went by in which Newton did not receive a report of someone coming to faith in Christ. A gallery was built to accommodate more pews as the congregation grew rapidly. While there was predictable resistance among some of the local inhabitants, there was a visible impact on everyday life in what was then one of the poorest towns in England.

It was Newton's habit to spend the early morning hours alone in his study, preparing his sermons, writing hymns and replying to the many letters he received requesting his wise pastoral counsel. His afternoons were generally spent with people.

> I believe I may say that for more than twenty years, very few single days have passed when … I did not spend from six to ten hours daily in subjects and employments which had a direct suitableness to pulpit service. I have written several perhaps I may say reams of paper in the forms of discourses, and for about ten or twelve years after I came to Olney, I seldom preached upon any text on which I had not previously written to some extent… [The] day seems rather lost and tedious if I have not had the opportunity of spending some hours with my pen in my hand, and the Bible open before me.
>
> (Quoted by Cecil, *John Newton*, p. 199)

> I have seldom one hour free from interruption. Letters come that must be answered, visitants that must be received, business that must be attended to. I have a good many sheep and lambs to look after, sick and afflicted souls, dear to the Lord; and therefore … these must not be neglected. Among these various avocations [i.e. occupations],

night comes before I am ready for noon; and the week
closes, when, according to the state of my business, it
should not be more than Tuesday.

(Quoted by Edwards, *Through Many Dangers*, p. 219)

On the subject of visits from Newton, Richard Cecil, a good
friend and a fellow minister, wrote, 'I do not recollect one, though
favoured with many, in which his general information and lively
genius did not communicate instruction, and his affectionate and
condescending sympathy did not leave comfort.'[2]

But for Newton (and for every true pastor) the pressures created
by weekly preparation and teaching and the demands of multiple
daily appointments were nothing compared with the ultimate strain
of pastoral ministry: the overwhelming, private concern for men's
souls. Newton knew at first hand the great joy of seeing people's
lives utterly transformed by the power of the gospel. But he also
experienced the unspeakable heartache of watching people he
loved ignore his pleadings from God's Word and make disobedient
choices that plunged their lives, often irreparably, into utter ruin and
destruction. He wrote a hymn in which he captured the unique joys
and burdens of the life of a minister of the gospel.

Travailing in birth for souls
Galatians 4:19.

*W*hat contradictions meet
In ministers' employ!
It is a bitter sweet,
A sorrow full of joy:
No other post affords a place
For equal honour, or disgrace!

Who can describe the pain
Which faithful preachers feel —
Constrained to speak, in vain,
To hearts as hard as steel?
Or who can tell the pleasures felt,
When stubborn hearts begin to melt?

The Saviour's dying love,
The soul's amazing worth,
Their utmost efforts move,
And draw their bowels [i.e. deepest emotions] forth:
They pray and strive, their rest departs,
Till Christ be formed in sinners' hearts.

If some small hope appear,
They still are not content;
But, with a jealous fear,
They watch for the event:
Too oft they find their hopes deceived,
Then, how their inmost souls are grieved!

But when their pains succeed,
And from the tender blade
The ripening ears proceed,
Their toils are overpaid:
No harvest-joy can equal theirs,
To find the fruit of all their cares.

On what has now been sown
Thy blessing, Lord, bestow;
The power is thine alone,
To make it spring and grow:
Do thou the gracious harvest raise,
And thou, alone, shalt have the praise.

                                   (*Olney Hymns,* Book 2, Hymn 26)

Those of my readers who are pastors will be both comforted and admonished by the further perspectives on pastoral ministry which follow. For other readers, I hope that these candid descriptions of the joys and heartaches of the gospel ministry will motivate you to pray for your own pastor and encourage you to make his ministry a joy rather than a burden!

A minister of the gospel ... has many [trials] peculiar to himself. His services are more difficult, his temptations more various, his conduct more noticed; many eyes are upon him — some enviously watching for his halting, and some perhaps too readily proposing him as a pattern, and content to adopt whatever has [the] sanction of his example. If encouraged and acceptable, he is in danger of being greatly hurt by popularity and the favour of friends; if opposed and ill-treated (and this he must expect in some instances if he is faithful), he is liable either to be surprised into anger or impatience, or to sink into dejection and fear.

(*A Review of Ecclesiastical History*, Chapter 2)

The ministers [of the gospel] are rejected, opposed, vilified; they are accounted troublers of the world, because they dare not, [they] cannot stand silent, while sinners are perishing before their eyes; and if, in the course of many sermons, they can prevail but on one soul to take timely warning, and to seek to Jesus, who is the way, the truth, and the life, they may account it a mercy and an honour, sufficient to overbalance all the labour and reproaches they are called to endure.

(*Cardiphonia*, 'Twenty-six Letters to a Nobleman', Letter 14)

To see his name made precious to the hearts of sinners; to see those who were blind admiring his excellency; to see those who were so far off from God brought so nigh; to see those who were wretched rejoicing in his goodness; to hear those whose lips were filled with folly, falsehood, or blasphemy proclaiming his praise; such salutary [i.e. beneficial] effects of their ministry fill them likewise with praise and joy; and when their hearers express the power and spirit of the gospel in their tempers and conduct, they can say, 'Now we live, if you stand fast in the Lord' (1 Thessalonians 3:8).

(*Fifty Sermons on Handel's 'The Messiah'*, Sermon 31)

In my judgement, he that does not find a reward in being excited, supported, enabled by the Holy Spirit of God in the work of the gospel, who does not think that to have multiplied labours owned [i.e. blessed by the Lord] to the conversion of even a few souls is a great reward, who does not account the ministry of the gospel, with grace to be faithful in the discharge of it, a reward and honour in itself sufficient to overbalance all the difficulties it may expose him to — whoever, I say does not thus think of the service to Jesus in the gospel, has some reason to question his right to the lowest degree of glory, or, at least, has little right to look for eminence in glory, even though he should preach with as much power and acceptance, and in the midst of as many hardships, as Paul did.

(*Cardiphonia*, 'Eighteen Letters to the Rev. Mr S…,' Letter 4)

Thus [God's] ministers are to declare his whole will, whether men will hear, or whether they shall forbear. And if they do this with a single eye to his glory, and in humble dependence upon his blessing, they are not answerable for the event; they shall in no wise lose their reward.

(*Twenty Sermons preached in the Parish Church of Olney*,
Sermon 1)

*S*uggested **Scripture readings**: Acts 20:17-38;
1 Thessalonians 2:1-9

'Obey your leaders and submit to them, for they keep watch over your souls… Let them do this with joy and not with grief, for this would be unprofitable for you' (Heb.13:17).

Advice to fellow ministers

As Newton aged, he became something of a patriarch of the Evangelical movement, investing more and more of his time in the next generation of pastors. In the words of Richard Cecil, 'Young ministers were peculiarly the objects of his attention; he instructed them; he encouraged them; he warned them: and might truly be said to be a father in Christ, spending and being spent, for the interest of his church.'[3]T

The story of Newton's influence in the life of a younger minister, Thomas Scott, is particularly fascinating. During Newton's years in Olney, Scott was the curate of nearby Ravenstone and Weston Underwood. Scott, who was a proud man, habitually ridiculed Evangelicals, including Newton, the minister of the neighbouring parish. Scott later described himself as being at that time 'full of proud self-sufficiency, very positive [i.e. self-confident], and very obstinate; and, being situated in the neighbourhood of some of those whom the world called Methodists [i.e. a pejorative term for Evangelicals], I joined in the prevailing sentiment; held them in sovereign contempt; spoke of them with derision; declaimed against them from the pulpit, as persons full of bigotry, enthusiasm [i.e. fanaticism], and spiritual pride; laid heavy things to their charge; and endeavoured to prove the doctrines which I supposed them to hold (for I never read their books) to be dishonourable to God and destructive to morality... Scarcely any person could be more proudly and violently prejudiced against both their persons and principles than I then was.'

He continues: 'In January, 1774, two of my parishioners, a man and his wife, lay at the point of death. I had heard of the circumstance; but, according to my general custom, not being sent for, I took no notice of it; till one evening, the woman being now dead, and the man dying, I heard that my neighbour, Mr [Newton], had been several times to visit them. Immediately my conscience reproached me with being shamefully negligent in sitting at home within a few doors of dying persons, my general hearers, and never going to visit them. Directly it occurred to me that, whatever contempt I might have for Mr N...'s *doctrines*, I must acknowledge his *practice* to be more consistent with ministerial conduct than my own. He must have more zeal and love for souls than I had, or he

Thomas Scott

would not have walked so far to visit, and supply my lack of care to those who, as far as I was concerned, might have been left to perish in their sins... It was at this time that my correspondence with Mr N... commenced.'[4]

So, under the guise of a desire for friendship, Scott began to exchange letters with Newton, always attempting to draw him into controversy, filling his own letters with definitions and arguments that required explicit answers. In response Newton sent him a copy of his book *Omicron*, while in his letters he purposely avoided controversy and focused on the gospel. After a few months, Scott stopped corresponding with Newton because he 'did not like his company... I was unwilling the world should think us connected in any way.'

But over a year later, when Scott was in need of friendship and encouragement, he re-established contact with Newton. The irresistible, persistent kindness of Newton began to humble Scott. Though still prejudiced, he began to come and listen to Newton preach. Slowly, Scott's heart was humbled and he came to believe that perhaps there was much he could learn from Newton not only about preaching, but also about what it meant to be a Christian.

Not long after Newton went to London, Scott was called to take up the post at Olney previously held by Newton. In a letter Newton wrote:

> Methinks I see you sitting in my old corner in the study. I
> will warn you of one thing, that room (do not start) used to

be haunted. I cannot say I ever saw or heard anything with my bodily organs, but I have been sure there were evil spirits in it and very near me — a spirit of folly, a spirit of indolence, a spirit of unbelief, and many others — indeed their name is legion. But why should I say they are in your study when they followed me to London, and still pester me here?

(Quoted by Edwards, *Through Many Dangers*, p.182)

Newton's diaries record many touching prayers for Scott, including the following:

Though his views were then very dark, and he objected to almost every point proposed, yet, I could perceive thou hast given him a sincerity, which I looked upon as a token of thy further favour. And now he seems enlightened and established in the most important truths of the gospel, and will I trust prove an instrument of usefulness in thy hand.

(Quoted by Cecil, *John Newton*, p. 324)

Newton's prayers for Scott's usefulness in gospel ministry were abundantly answered! Some years later Scott, like Newton himself, eventually left Olney to preach in London. Wilberforce regularly went to hear him preach and Richard Cecil, an eminent preacher in London who occasionally asked Scott to fill his pulpit, found that he could not repress whispered bursts of admiration while listening to him. Scott went on to publish his *Practical Commentary on the Bible*. He was influential in founding the British and Foreign Bible Society; he trained other ministers and missionaries and played a key role in influencing the theology of William Carey. Scott's three sons went on to be ministers as well.

However, it was not only fellow Anglicans like Scott, but also Dissenters, Baptists and Methodists who sought advice from the wise and experienced Rev. John Newton. Some of these men had the privilege of attending morning family worship in the Newton home in London, which was followed by a time of informal questions and answers. One of those who were privileged to attend these breakfast gatherings wrote, '… the good old man, in his velvet cap and damask dressing-gown, was then fresh and communicative, always instructive, always benevolent. His expositions of Scripture with his family, which consisted of niece [Betsy], some aged servants, and some poor blind inmates of his house, were peculiarly simple and devout.'⁵

Others received counsel from Newton in the form of a personal letter. Whatever the venue and whatever the theological persuasion of the person seeking his help, everyone was sure to receive equally warm, straightforward and practical advice from a man who was passionate about the high calling of the Christian ministry. In one such letter, he discusses the question of academic preparation for the ministry:

> My first maxim is that none but the one who made the world can make a minister of the gospel. If a young man has capacity, [then] culture and application may make him a scholar, a philosopher, or an orator; but a true minister must have certain principles, motives, feelings, and aims, which no industry or endeavours of men can either acquire or communicate. They must be given from above, or they cannot be received...
>
> I adopt, as a second maxim, that the Holy Scriptures are, both comprehensively and exclusively, the grand treasury of all that knowledge which is requisite and sufficient to make the minister the man of God, thoroughly furnished for every branch of his office...

Describing the qualities needed in one who is to train men for the ministry, he continues:

> For his first essential, indispensable qualification, I require a mind deeply penetrated with a sense of the grace, glory, and efficacy of the gospel. However learned and able in other respects, he shall not have a single pupil from me, unless I have reason to believe that his heart is attached to the person of the Redeemer, as God-man; that, as a sinner, his whole dependence is upon the Redeemer's work of love, his obedience unto death, his intercession and mediatorial

fulness. His sentiments must be clear and explicit respecting
the depravity of human nature, and the necessity and reality of the agency of the Holy Spirit, to quicken, enlighten,
sanctify, and seal those who, under his influence, are led to
Jesus for salvation...

I should look for my tutor among those who are called
Calvinists; but he must not be of a curious, metaphysical,
disputatious [i.e. argumentative] turn [of mind], a mere
system-monger or party-zealot. I seek for one who, having
been himself taught the deep things of God by the Holy
Spirit, in a gradual experimental manner; while he is
charmed with the beautiful harmony and coincidence [i.e.
interdependence] of all the doctrines of grace, is at the same
time aware of the mysterious depths of the divine counsels,
and the impossibility of [their] being fully apprehended by
our feeble understandings. Such a man will be patient and
temperate in explaining the peculiarities [i.e. the distinctive
features] of the gospel to his students, and will wisely adapt
himself to their several states, attainments, and capacities.

(*A Plan for Academic Preparation for the Ministry*)

The letter quoted below was written to a young minister who had
requested Newton's thoughts on the occasion of his ordination. I am
sure that any pastors reading this book will heartily endorse every
word of the letter and perhaps will also be comforted by Newton's
candour regarding the struggles he faced, both in the study and in
the pulpit. I also hope that other readers will be motivated by
Newton's words to pray more earnestly for their own pastor in the
unique temptations that he faces in ministry.

You have, doubtless, often anticipated in your mind the
nature of the service to which you are now called, and
made it the subject of much consideration and prayer. But
a distant view of the ministry is generally very different
from what it is found to be when we are actually engaged
in it. The young soldier, who has never seen an enemy,

may form some general notions of what is before him; but his ideas will be much more lively and diversified when he comes upon the field of battle. If the Lord was to show us the whole beforehand, who, that has a due sense of his own insufficiency and weakness, would venture to engage [in it]? But he first draws us by a constraining sense of his love, and by giving us an impression of the worth of souls, and leaves us to acquire a knowledge of what is difficult and disagreeable by a gradual experience. The ministry of the gospel, like the book which the apostle John ate, is a bitter sweet; but the sweetness is tasted first, the bitterness is usually known afterwards, when we are so far engaged that there is no going back...

You have known something of Satan's devices while you were in private life... But you may now expect to hear from him, and to be beset by his power and subtlety in a different manner. You are now to be placed in the forefront of the battle, and to stand as it were for his mark [i.e. target]. So far as he can prevail against you now, not yourself only, but many others will be affected. Many eyes will be upon you; and if you take a wrong step, or are ensnared into a wrong spirit, you will open the mouths of the adversaries wider, and grieve the hearts of believers more sensibly [i.e. more deeply] than if the same things happened to you while you were a layman...

If opposition has hurt many, popularity has wounded more. To say the truth, I am in some pain for you. Your natural abilities are considerable; you have been diligent in your studies; your zeal is warm, and your spirit is lively. With these advantages, I expect to see you a popular preacher. The more you are so, the greater will your field of usefulness be; but, alas! you cannot yet know to what it will expose you. It is like walking upon ice. When you shall see an attentive congregation hanging upon your words; when you shall hear the well-meant, but often injudicious, commendations of those to whom the Lord shall make you useful; when you shall find, upon an intimation of your preaching in a strange place, people thronging from all parts to hear you — how will your heart feel? It is easy for me to advise you to be humble, and for you to acknowledge the propriety of the advice; but while human nature remains in its present state, there will be almost the same connection between popularity and pride as between fire and gunpowder: they cannot meet without an explosion, at least not unless the gunpowder is kept very damp. So, unless the Lord is constantly moistening our hearts (if I may so speak) by the influences of his Spirit, popularity will soon set us in a blaze...

Beware, my friend, of mistaking the ready exercise of gifts for the exercise of grace. The minister may be assisted in public for the sake of his hearers; and there is something in the nature of our public work, when surrounded by a concourse of people, that is suited to draw forth the exertion of our abilities, and to engage our attention in the outward services, when the frame of heart may be far from being right in the sight of the Lord...

Many distressing exercises you will probably meet with upon the best supposition, to preserve in you a due sense of your own unworthiness, and to convince you that your ability, your acceptance, and your usefulness depend upon a power beyond your own. Sometimes, perhaps, you will feel such an amazing difference between the frame of your spirit in public and in private, when the eyes of men are not upon you, as will make you almost ready to conclude that you are no better than a hypocrite, a mere stage-player, who derives all his pathos and exertion from the sight of the audience. At other times you will find such a total emptiness and indisposition of mind that former seasons of liberty in preaching will appear to you like the remembrance of a dream, and you will hardly be able to persuade yourself you shall ever be capable of preaching again: the Scriptures will appear to you like a sealed book, and no text or subject afford any light or opening to determine your choice. And this perplexity may not only seize you in the study, but accompany you in the pulpit... So that you need not tell the people you have no sufficiency in yourself; for they will readily perceive it without your information. These things are hard to bear; yet successful popularity is not to be preserved upon easier terms; and if they are but sanctified to hide pride from you, you will have reason to number them amongst your choicest mercies.

> (*Forty-one Letters on Religious Subjects*, Letter 5)

Below are a collection of miscellaneous comments, some of them witty, by Newton on pastoral ministry.

I measure ministers by square measure. I have no idea of the size of a table, if you only tell me how *long* it is; but if you also say how *wide*, I can tell its dimensions. So when you tell me what a man is in the pulpit, you must also tell me what he is out of it, or I shall not know his size.

> (Quoted by Edwards, *Through Many Dangers*, p.174)

A minister, wherever he is, should always be in his study. He should look at every man, and at every thing, as capable of affording him some instruction.

> (Quoted by Cecil, *John Newton*, p. 192)

When we read [sermons] to the people, they think themselves less concerned in what is offered than when we speak to them point blank.

> (Quoted by Cecil, *John Newton*, p.199)

Overlong sermons break in upon family concerns, and often call thoughts from the sermon to the pudding at home, which is danger of being over-boiled.

(Quoted by Edwards, *Through Many Dangers*, p.175)

Suggested **Scripture readings:** 2 Timothy 1:13 – 2:10

'The things which you have heard from me in the presence of many witnesses, entrust these to faithful men who will be able to teach others also' (2 Tim. 2:2).

Nuggets of wisdom

A selection of conversational gems

Richard Cecil closed his biography of Newton with a section entitled 'Remarks made by Mr Newton in Familiar Conversation', which were 'taken down at different times, both in company and in private, from his lips'. They not only demonstrate the breadth of subjects on which Newton offered his seemingly endless down-to-earth advice, but also reveal a warm, lively sense of humour. Here are some of my favourites from these 'nuggets of wisdom':

> If two angels came down from heaven to execute a divine command, and one was appointed to conduct an empire, and the other to sweep a street in it, they would feel no inclination to change employments.

> A Christian should never plead spirituality for being a sloven [i.e. for being slovenly]; if he be but a shoe-cleaner, he should be the best in the parish.

> Many have puzzled themselves about the origin of evil: I observe there *is* evil, and that there is a way to escape it; and with this I begin and end.

A spirit of adoption is the spirit of a child: he may dis-oblige [i.e. go against the wishes of] his father, yet he is not afraid of being turned out of doors. The *union* is not dis-solved, though the *communion* is. He is not well [i.e. on good terms] with his father; therefore must be unhappy, as their interests are inseparable.

There are critical times of danger. After great services, honours, and consolations, we should stand upon our guard. Noah, Lot, David, Solomon fell in these circum-stances. Satan is a robber: a robber will not attack a man in *going* to the bank, but in *returning* with his pocket full of money.

I remember, in going to undertake the care of a congre-gation, I was reading as I walked in a green lane, 'Fear not, Paul, I have much people in this city.' But I soon afterwards was disappointed in finding that Paul was not John [New-ton] and that Corinth was not Warwick.

Christ has taken our nature into heaven, to represent *us*; and he has left us on earth, with his nature, to represent *him*.

The Scriptures are so full that every case may be found in them. A rake [i.e. a man known for his dissolute lifestyle] went into a church, and tried to decoy a girl by saying, 'Why do you attend to such stuff as these Scriptures?' 'Be-cause,' said she, 'they tell me that, in the last days, there shall come such scoffers as you.'

Some preachers near Olney dwelt on the doctrine of predestination. An old woman said, 'Ah! I have long settled that point: for, if God had not chosen me before I was born, I am sure he would have seen nothing in me to have chosen me afterwards.'

The heir of a great estate, while a child, thinks more of a few shillings in his pocket than of his inheritance. So a Christian is often more elated by some frame of heart than by his title to glory.

I have read of many wicked popes, but the worst pope I ever met with is Pope Self.

Man is capable of three births: by nature, he enters into the present world; by grace, into spiritual light and life; by death, into glory.

In my imagination, I sometimes fancy I could make a perfect minister. I take the eloquence of [A], the knowledge of [B], the zeal of [C], and the pastoral meekness, tenderness, and piety of [D]: then, putting them all together into one man, I say to myself, '*This* would be a perfect minister.' Now there is one, who, if he chose it, could actually *do* this; but he never did. He has seen fit to do otherwise, and to divide these gifts 'to every man severally as he will'.
(*Memoirs of the Rev. John Newton,* chapter 10, 'Remarks made by Mr Newton in familiar conversation')

S uggested **Scripture readings:** Proverbs 9:8-9; 29:9-11

'*A joyful heart is good medicine, but a broken spirit dries up the bones*' (Prov. 17:22).

5.

HOPE BEYOND THE GRAVE

More light, more love, more liberty —
hereafter I hope, when I shut my eyes
on the things of time, I shall open them
in a better world. What a thing it is
to live under the shadow of the wings of
the Almighty!

JOHN NEWTON
DIED 21ST DECR 1807
AGED 82

MARY NEWTON
DIED 15TH DECR 1790
AGED 61

John Newton's tomb at Olney

On the loss of a loved one

What a change is before me!

Below are excerpts from a tract written by Newton which paid tribute to the vibrant testimony of Eliza Cunningham, Mary Newton's niece. The Newtons took Eliza into their home when she was twelve years old, following the death of her entire family from tuberculosis. By the time she moved to the Newtons' home in London, she was already ill herself with the disease. The entire Newton household delighted in caring for the attractive, cheerful and intelligent young girl, who was not yet a Christian. The Lord worked in Eliza's heart as she listened to her Uncle John's public preaching and as he led the daily family worship. Newton records that the Lord graciously 'enlightened her understanding and had drawn the desires of her heart to him' before her death at the age of fourteen.

Newton preached her funeral sermon on the text Eliza herself had selected: 'Blessed are the dead who die in the Lord' (Revelation 14:13). She also requested that Newton lead the congregation in the hymn entitled 'Hope Beyond the Grave' which he had written some years earlier. He subsequently wrote a tract entitled *A Monument to the Praise of the Lord's Goodness and to the Memory of Dear Eliza Cunningham*, which was widely circulated as an evangelistic tool throughout London. Eliza's confidence provides a shining example for any reader who may be suffering, or facing death, and Newton's response to her death is an excellent model of unselfishness in the midst of grief.

She said to me about ten o'clock, 'My dear uncle, I would not change conditions with any person upon earth. Oh, how gracious is the Lord to me! Oh, what a change is before me!' She was several times asked if she could wish to live, provided the Lord should restore her to perfect health. Her answer was, 'Not for all the world,' and sometimes, 'Not for a thousand worlds. Do not weep for me, my dear aunt; but rather rejoice and praise on my account.' ...

She had something to say, either in the way of admonition or consolation, as she thought most suitable, to everyone whom she saw. To her most constant attendant, she said, 'Be sure you continue to call upon the Lord; and, if you think he does not hear you now, he will at last, as he has heard me.' She spoke a great deal to an intimate friend, who was with her every day, which I hope she will long remember, as the testimony of her dying Eliza. Among other things she said, 'See how comfortable the Lord can make a dying-bed! Do you think that you shall have such an assurance when you come to die?' Being answered, 'I hope so, my dear,' she replied, 'But do you earnestly, and with all your heart, pray to the Lord for it? If you seek him, you shall surely find him.' She then prayed affectionately and fervently for her friend, afterwards for her cousin, and then for another of our family who was present. Her prayer was not long, but every word was weighty, and her manner very affecting; the purport was that they might all be taught and comforted by the Lord. About five in the afternoon she desired me to pray with her once more. Surely I then prayed from my heart. When I had finished, she said 'Amen'. I said, 'My dear child, have I expressed your meaning?' She answered, 'Oh yes!' and then added, 'I am ready to say, "Why are his chariot wheels so long in coming?" But

I hope he will enable me to wait his hour with patience.' These were the last words I heard her speak...

Towards seven o'clock, I was walking in the garden, and earnestly engaged in prayer for her, when a servant came to me, and said, 'She is gone.' O Lord, how great is thy power! How great is thy goodness! A few days before, had it been practicable and lawful, what would I not have given to procure her recovery? Yet seldom in my life have I known a more heartfelt joy than when these words, 'She is gone,' sounded in my ears. I ran upstairs and our whole little family were soon around her bed... She lay upon her left side, with her cheek gently reclining upon her hand, as if in a sweet sleep. And I thought there was a smile on her countenance. Never, surely, did death appear in a more beautiful, inviting form!

We fell upon our knees, and I returned (I think I may say) my most unfeigned thanks to our God and Saviour, for his abundance goodness to her, crowned in this last instance, by giving her so gentle a dismission [i.e. passing]. Yes, I am satisfied and comforted... Now my largest desires for her are accomplished. The days of her mourning are ended. She is landed on that peaceful shore, where the storms of trouble never blow. She is for ever out of the reach of sorrow, sin, temptation, and snares. Now she is before the throne! She sees him whom, not having seen, she loved; she drinks of the rivers of pleasure which are at his right hand, and shall thirst no more.

(*A Monument to the Praise of the Lord's Goodness and to the Memory of Dear Eliza Cunningham*)

Hope beyond the grave

M y soul, this curious house of clay,
   Thy present frail abode,
Must quickly fall to worms a prey,
And thou return to God.

Canst thou, by faith, survey with joy
The change, before it come?
And say, 'Let death this house destroy,
I have a heavenly home!'

The Saviour, whom I then shall see
With new admiring eyes,
Already has prepared for me
A mansion in the skies.

I feel this mud-walled cottage shake,
And long to see it fall;
That I my willing flight may take
To him who is my all.

Burdened and groaning, then no more,
My rescued soul shall sing,
As up the shining path I soar,
'Death, thou hast lost thy sting.'

Dear Saviour, help us now to seek,
And know thy grace's power;
That we may all this language speak,
Before the dying hour.

(*Olney Hymns*, Book 2, Hymn 75)

S uggested Scripture readings: Psalm 16:1-11; Revelation
21:1-8

'*Precious in the sight of the LORD is the death of his godly ones*'
(Ps. 116:16).

Yet I will rejoice in the Lord

When Newton was seventeen years old, he received an invitation to visit the Catlett family, who had been extremely close friends of his mother and had in fact cared for her in their home in her last illness. The Catletts, disapproving of the hasty remarriage of Newton's father, had made no contact with the Newtons for a decade. Not having been close to the family, Newton was indifferent about accepting the invitation, but he did pay them a visit. It turned out to be one of the most important visits he ever made in his life. The Catletts had two daughters, the older of whom was named Mary (although she was known in the family as Polly, and this was Newton's usual name for her). Newton recalled meeting her for the first time:

> Almost at the first sight of this girl (for she was then under fourteen), I was impressed with an affection for her, which never abated or lost its influence a single moment in my heart from that hour. In degree, it actually equalled all that the writers of romance have imagined; in duration it was unalterable.
>
> (*An Authentic Narrative*, Letter 3).

Newton was later to learn that ever since she was born, Mary had been considered by both their mothers as a future wife for him.

Newton's early affection for Mary was so intense that on two different occasions he intentionally protracted his visits to her family in order to avoid his father's plans to set him up in business in Jamaica for a period of four to five years, since he could not bear the thought of being apart from her for so long. Later, having been pressed into service in the navy, he went 'absent without leave' because of his strong desire to see Mary. Newton explained how the Lord providentially used his deep love for Mary to keep him from taking his own life at the lowest point of his moral decay:

> I soon lost all sense of religion and became deaf to the remonstrances of conscience and prudence: but my regard

for her was always the same; and I may perhaps venture to say that none of the scenes of misery and wickedness I afterward experienced ever banished her [for] a single hour together from my waking thoughts for seven years following.

My love [for Mary] was now the only restraint I had left; though I neither feared God nor regarded man, I could not bear that *she* should think meanly of me when I was dead.

(*An Authentic Narrative*, Letters 3, 4)

Following Newton's conversion, the couple were married, some seven years after their initial meeting. Newton expressed gratitude that the Lord had kept them from marrying before he became a Christian:

I had renounced my former follies, my interest was established, and friends on all sides consenting, the point was now entirely between ourselves, and, after what had passed, was easily concluded. Accordingly, our hands were joined on the first of February 1750.

The satisfaction I have found in this union, you will suppose, has been greatly heightened by reflections on the former disagreeable contrasts I had passed through, and the views I have had of the singular mercy and providence of the Lord in bringing it to pass... How easily, at a time of life when I was so little capable of judgement (but a few months more than seventeen), might my affections have been fixed where they could have met with no return, or the heaviest disappointment. The long delay that I met with was likewise a mercy; for, had I succeeded a year or two sooner, before the Lord was pleased to change my heart, we must have been mutually unhappy, even as to the present life.

(*An Authentic Narrative*, Letter 11)

Mary, in spite of her somewhat frail health, ministered by Newton's side without complaint. Their marriage was a true partnership in the gospel, a true ministry on the part of both husband and wife. Together they weathered the joys and disappointments of pastoral ministry; together they raised their adopted niece Betsy; together they showed warm hospitality to others, regularly opening their home to encourage and instruct friends and young ministers, and making it a haven for the poor, the afflicted and fragile, spiritually needy people.

After almost forty-one years of marriage, their happy union was ended. On Wednesday, 15 December 1790, a little before ten in the evening, Mary died of breast cancer, with her devoted husband at her bedside keeping vigil by candlelight. The loss was catastrophic for Newton, who often confessed that he feared his love for Mary was so great that it might border on idolatry. However, believing that God uses trials in a minister's life to display his own glory, he was enabled by God's grace to preach her funeral sermon a few days later, on Sunday, 26 December. He preached from Habakkuk 3:17-18, a text on which he had never previously spoken, having reserved it years earlier with the possibility of this very event in mind, in case Mary should predecease him. Following the sermon, Newton had the congregation sing a new hymn he had written based on this special text.

Verses sung after her funeral sermon

Habakkuk 3:17,18

> *Although the fig-tree shall not blossom, neither shall fruit be in the vines; the labour of the olive shall fail, and the fields shall yield no meat; the flock shall be cut off from the fold, and there shall be no herd in the stalls: yet I will rejoice in the LORD, I will joy in the God of my salvation.*

*T*he earth, with rich abundance stored
  To answer all our wants,
Invites our hearts to praise the Lord
For what his bounty grants.

Flocks, herds, and corn, and grateful fruit,
His gracious hand supplies;
And, while our various tastes they suit,
Their prospect cheers our eyes.

To these he adds each tender tie
Of sweet domestic life;
Endearing joys, the names imply,
Of parent, husband, wife!

But sin has poisoned all below,
Our blessings burdens prove;
On every hand we suffer woe,
But most where most we love.

Nor vintage, harvest, flocks, nor herds,
Can fill the heart's desire;
And oft a worm destroys our gourds [see Jonah 4],
And all our hopes expire.

Domestic joys, alas! how rare!
Possessed, and known by few!
And those who know them find they are
As frail and transient too.

But you, who love the Saviour's voice,
And rest upon his name,
Amidst these changes may rejoice,
For he is still the same.

The Lord himself will soon appear,
Whom you, unseen, adore;
Then he will wipe off every tear,
And you shall weep no more.

Newton preserved the memory of his love for Mary and their
exceptionally blessed marriage in several ways.

In the first place, he published *Letters to a Wife*, a collection of
personal correspondence written during his long voyages to Africa
in the early days of their marriage, together with letters sent to her
from Liverpool and Olney, whenever it was necessary for them to be

apart. He said in his preface to the letters, 'Some testimony in favour of the happiness of wedded life, some intimation of the snares and abatements which attend it seems not unseasonable in the present day. And perhaps I am, by experience, qualified to be as unexceptionable a witness, in both respects, as most men.'

Secondly, for the remainder of his life, on the anniversary of Mary's death Newton spent the day in seclusion for meditation and prayer.

Thirdly, during those annual days of seclusion, he gave expression to his grief through poems composed on the first five anniversaries of Mary's death. These extremely intimate, moving poems record details of the last days, even the final moments, of his wife's life. They also serve to trace the steady progress made by Newton's grieving heart. These poems, from which excerpts are quoted below, exemplify the difference between mere resignation and joyful submission to the will of God, painful though this may often be.

First anniversary of the 15th of December

L ord! She was thine and not my own;
    Thou hast not done me wrong;
I thank thee for the precious loan
Afforded me so long.

For, though no single day had been,
Or talent, well-improved [i.e. put to good use];
I chiefly see, and mourn, my sin,
In what I chiefly loved.

I trembled when thou saidst, 'Resign
A much abused trust',
But could not wonder or repine;
I owned the sentence just.

Yet mercy sweetened my distress;
And while I felt the rod,

Gave me abundant cause to bless
An all-sufficient God!

Sharp was my pain and deep my wound
(A wound which still must bleed);
But daily help and strength I found,
Proportioned to my need.

Like Jonah (well our stories suit),
I viewed my gourd, well pleased;
Like him, I could not see the root
On which the worm had seized.

But saw, at length, the hour draw nigh,
(That hour I since have known)
When all my earthly joy must die,
And I be left alone.

She dropped a tear, and grasped my hand,
And fain she would have spoke;
But well my heart could understand
The language of her look.

'Farewell,' it meant, a last adieu!
'I soon shall cease from pain;
This silent tear I drop for you;
We part — to meet again.'

I said, 'If leaving all below,
You now have peace divine;
And would, but cannot tell me so,
Give me at least a sign.'

She raised, and gently waved her hand
And filled me with a joy,

To which the wealth of sea and land
Compared would be a toy.

I trust, indeed, she knew thy grace,
Before this trying day;
But Satan had, a while, access,
To fill her with dismay.

Till then, though two long years she pined [i.e. suffered]
Without an hour of ease,
Cheerful, she still appeared resigned,
And bore her cross in peace.

Daily, while able, closely too,
She read the Word of God;
And thence her hope and comfort drew,
Her med'cine and her food.

A stranger might have well presumed
From what he saw her bear;
This burning bush was not consumed
Because the Lord was there.

Three days, she could no notice take,
Not speak, nor hear, nor see;
O Lord, did not my heart-strings ache?
Did not I cry to thee?

That, while I watched her night and day,
My will to thine might bow?
And, by this rod, didst thou not say,
'Behold, your idol now'?

'From her you loved too much, proceed
Your sharpest grief and pains;

For, soon or late, the heart must bleed
That idol entertains.'

Yes, Lord, we both have guilty been,
And justly are distressed;
But, since thou dost forgive our sin,
I welcome all the rest.

Only uphold us in the fire,
Our fainting spirits cheer;
And I thy mercy will admire,
When most thou seem'st severe.

Fainter her breath, and fainter, grew,
Until she breathed her last;
The soul was gone before we knew
The stroke of death had passed.

Soft was the moment, and serene,
That all her sufferings closed;
No agony or struggle seen,
No feature discomposed.

The parting struggle all was mine.
'Tis the survivor dies:
For she was freed, and gone to join
The triumph of the skies.

To me it was a stormy day,
Though glad for her release;
But he whom seas and storms obey
Soon bid the tempest cease.

My selfish heart had wished her here,
To spend her days in pain;

That she what I could say might hear,
And speak to me again.

Our kindness to our suff'ring friends
Would keep them still below;
But he who loves them better, sends,
And at his call they go.

Each moment, since that trying hour,
My loss I keenly feel;
And trust, I feel, my Saviour's power
To sanctify and heal.

Ah, world, vain world! by whom my Lord
Was crucified and slain,
What comfort now canst thou afford
To mitigate my pain?

Long since, I should, by his dear cross,
Have learnt to die to thee;
But, if I learn it by my loss,
That loss my gain shall be.

Now, Lord, to thee I would apply,
On thee alone depend;
Thou art, when creatures fail and die,
An ever-living Friend!

Now thou hast made a void within,
Which only thou canst fill:
Oh, grant me pardon of my sin,
And grace to do thy will!

That I with joy thy flock may feed,
A pattern to them be,

And comfort them in time of need,
Vouchsafe to comfort me.

Let me believe, and love, and praise,
And wonder and adore,
And view thee guiding all my ways;
I ask for nothing more.

To thee I would commit the rest;
The when, the how, the where;
Thy wisdom will determine best,
Without my anxious care.

May I with faith and patience wait,
For soon thy call will come;
When I shall change this mortal state
For an eternal home.

The veils of sin and unbelief
Shall then be rent in twain;
And those who parted here with grief
Shall meet, with joy, again.

Then will the Lord himself appear,
With all his blood-bought sheep,
To wipe from every face the tear,
And they no more shall weep.

May thoughts like these relieve my toil,
And cheer my spirit up!
Who would not suffer here a while,
For such a glorious hope?

Second anniversary of the 15th of December

S hall one so favoured e'er repine?
   Or one so vile complain?
No, let me praise — she long was mine,
And shall be mine again.
If death could break our union past,
(Frail, though endeared, the tie),
The stronger band of grace shall last,
When death itself shall die!

Third anniversary of the 15th of December

E nough with the language of sense,
   Still harping on sorrow and death;
I turn my attention from thence,
To hear the glad tidings of faith!
For faith has intuitive skill
(Believers best know what I mean)
To pierce through the veil at her will,
And realize objects unseen.

A glimpse of the throne she obtains,
Which all the redeemèd surround;
And catches some notes of the strains
Which through the glad regions resound.
That moment the earth is forgot,
Its trifles she then can despise;
No more she complains of her lot,
But joins in the praise of the skies…

I grieved while I saw her distressed,
By Satan, by sickness, and pain;
But now she possesses her rest,
And never will sorrow again…

Yet surely, when yonder we meet,
And with him [i.e. Christ] in glory appear,
We shall not, we cannot, forget
The mercies afforded us here;
How first he enriched us with love,
More precious than mountains of pelf [i.e. money];
Then raised our affections above,
To seek our best joys in himself.

Fourth anniversary of the 15th of December

Forget her? No. Can four short years
The deep impression wear away?
She still before my mind appears,
Abroad, at home, by night, by day.

Oft as with those she loved I meet,
Her looks, her voice, her words recur;
Or if alone I walk the street,
Still something leads my thoughts to her.

What she desired, while yet alive,
Has all the force of law to me;
It is my joy to watch and strive
That nothing may neglected be.

While thus self-pleased, my conscience spoke,
And roused me from my soothing dream:
'Vain worm, regard my just rebuke,
Nor longer glory in your shame! …

'Her dying words are not forgot,
Are his [Christ's] as constantly in view,
A law and rule to every thought,
To what you say and what you do?' …

Well may this charge my spirit sink!
Thy mercy, Lord, is all my plea!
How vile and base am I to think
So much of her, no more of thee!

Fifth anniversary of the 15th of December

*T*he Lord has healed the wound he made,
    And caused my grief to end:
How weak was I to be afraid
Of such a faithful Friend!

I trembled when I saw the knife;
I knew my heart must bleed;
I would have prayed, 'Oh, spare my wife!
This is a wound indeed!'

But soon his tenderness and skill
Relieved me from alarm:
He cut, but cheered me with a smile,
And bid me fear no harm.

From him who died, my soul to save
From sin's desert [i.e. just deserts] and doom,
Who gave me all I had, or have,
Surely no harm can come.

What he appoints, I now perceive,
Is all in mercy sent;
My part is only to believe,
Submit and be content.

Content! That word's too faint to use,
I should, I *do* rejoice;
Unable for myself to choose,
I glory in his choice.

From many cares and fears, my mind
Was by the stroke set free;
It broke the ties which much confined
My thoughts, vain world, to thee.

Now, as on rising ground I stand,
Reviewing what is past;
I see that love and wisdom planned
My path from first to last.

Then let me change my sighs to praise,
For all that he has done;
And yield my few remaining days
To him and him alone.

I hope to join her soon again,
On yonder happy shore,
Where neither sorrow, sin, nor pain
Shall ever reach us more.

(Letters to a Wife, Appendix 2)

Suggested **Scripture readings:** Habakkuk 3:17-19;
Ephesians 5:22-33

'*Yet I will rejoice in the LORD; I will take joy in the God of my salvation*' (Hab. 3:18, ESV).

Newton's final days

Waiting for the post

At the age of eighty, though virtually blind, Newton was still preaching. When his close friend and biographer, Richard Cecil, suggested that he might consider that it was time to stop, Newton replied, raising his voice, 'I cannot stop. What! Shall the old African blasphemer stop while he can speak?' However, less than two years after that statement Newton was bedridden. He spent the last eleven months of his life confined to his room, tenderly cared for by his niece Betsy and her husband Joseph Smith.

Newton made his last journal entry on 21 March 1805, the anniversary of the violent Atlantic storm that the Lord had used to begin his spiritual awakening. He had made it his annual custom to spend that day in grateful prayer and meditation, and this day, exactly two years and nine months before his death, was no exception. He wrote, 'Not well able to write, but I endeavour to observe the return of this day with humiliation, prayer, and praise.'[1] Though no longer able to participate in conversation because of the loss of his hearing, Newton was alert until his last hour. His characteristic spiritual-mindedness, personal humility and robust confidence in Christ are evident in the following statements made in his final days:

> It is a great thing to die; and when our flesh and heart fail, to have God for the strength of our heart, and our portion for ever — I know whom I have believed, and he is able

to keep that which I have committed against that great day. Henceforth there is laid up for me a crown of righteousness, which the Lord, the righteous Judge, shall give me at that day.

[To his niece Betsy he said], I have been meditating on a subject, 'Come and hear, all ye that fear God, and I will declare what he hath done for my soul.'

[When someone reminded Newton of the graciousness of the Lord, he replied], If it were not so, how could I dare to stand before him?

[The Wednesday before he died, when asked if his mind was comfortable he replied], I am satisfied with the Lord's will.

(Quoted by Cecil, *John Newton*, pp.164-5)

More light, more love, more liberty – hereafter I hope, when I shut my eyes on the things of time, I shall open them in a better world. What a thing it is to live under the shadow of the wings of the Almighty! I am going the way of all flesh.

I am like a person going a journey in a stage coach, who expects its arrival every hour, and is frequently looking out the window for it.

I am packed and sealed and waiting for the post.

My memory is nearly gone; but I remember two things: that I am a great sinner and that Christ is a great Saviour.

(Quoted by Edwards, *Through Many Dangers*, pp. 347-8)

John Newton died at his home on 21 December 1807 with his dear Betsy at his side. He was buried beside his wife Mary and their niece Eliza Cunningham in the vault of his church, St Mary Woolnoth in London, where he had faithfully preached the Word of God for twenty-eight years. Newton had written the following epitaph, and requested that this, and nothing else, should be engraved on a plain marble tablet and mounted near the vestry door:

JOHN NEWTON,

CLERK

ONCE AN INFIDEL AND LIBERTINE,

A SERVANT OF SLAVES IN AFRICA,

WAS,

BY THE RICH MERCY

OF OUR LORD AND SAVIOUR

JESUS CHRIST,

PRESERVED, RESTORED, PARDONED,

AND APPOINTED TO PREACH THE FAITH

HE HAD LONG LABOURED TO DESTROY.

HE MINISTERED

NEAR XVI YEARS AS CURATE AND VICAR

OF *OLNEY* IN *BUCKS;*

AND XXVIII AS RECTOR OF THESE UNITED PARISHES.

ON FEBRY. THE FIRST MDCCL [1750}, HE MARRIED

MARY,

DAUGHTER OF THE LATE GEORGE CATLETT

OF *CHATHAM, KENT,*

WHOM HE RESIGNED

TO THE LORD WHO GAVE HER,

ON DEC^R. THE XVTH MDCCXC [1790]

Later, Newton's remains, along with those of Mary, were reinterred in the graveyard at Olney.

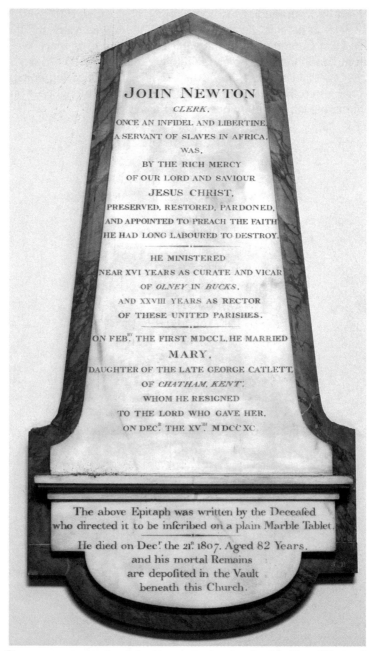

Plaque commemorating John Newton in the church of St Mary Woolnoth

On the death of a believer

*I*n vain my fancy strives to paint
  The moment after death;
The glories that surround the saints,
When yielding up their breath.

One gentle sigh their fetters breaks,
We scarce can say, 'They're gone!'
Before the willing spirit takes
Her mansion near the throne.

Faith strives, but all its efforts fail,
To trace her in her flight:
No eye can pierce within the veil
Which hides that world of light.

Thus much (and this is all) we know,
They are completely blest;
Have done with sin, and care, and woe,
And with their Saviour rest.

On harps of gold they praise his name,
His face they always view;
Then let us followers be of them,
That we may praise him too.

Their faith and patience, love and zeal,
Should make their memory dear;
And, Lord, do thou the prayers fulfil,
They offered for us here!

While they have gained, we losers are,
We miss them day by day;
But thou canst every breach repair,
And wipe our tears away.

We pray, as in Elisha's case,
When great Elijah went,
May double portions of thy grace
To us, who stay, be sent.

(*Olney Hymns,* Book 2, Hymn 72)

Suggested **Scripture readings:** 2 Timothy 4:6-8; Philippians 1:21-30

'I have fought the good fight, I have finished the course, I have kept the faith' (2 Tim. 4:7).

Bibliography

Unless otherwise noted, all quotations from the writings of John Newton are taken from *The Works of John Newton*, published by The Banner of Truth Trust, Edinburgh, 1988.

The following works have also been helpful:

John Newton by Richard Cecil, updated by Marylynn Rouse (Christian Focus Publications, Fearn, Ross-shire, 2000).

Through Many Dangers by Brian Edwards (Evangelical Press, Darlington, revised and enlarged edition, 2001).

John Newton and the Evangelical Tradition by D. Bruce Hindmarsh (Eerdmans' Publishing, Grand Rapids / Cambridge, 2001).

Notes

Introduction
1. John Newton, *An Authentic Narrative of Some Remarkable and Interesting Particulars in the Life of...,* letter 2.
2. Josiah Bull, *But Now I See, The Life of John Newton,* Banner of Truth, p.363.

1. So great salvation
1. D. Bruce Hindmarsh, *John Newton and the Evangelical Tradition,* Eerdmans' Publishing,, Grand Rapids, p.90.
2. As above, p.98.
3. As above, p.168.
4. As above, p.64.
5. Richard Cecil, *John Newton* (updated by Marylynn Rouse), Christian Focus Publications, Fearn, Ross-shire, 2000, p.125.
6. As above, p,130.
7. As above, p,129.

2. Growing in holiness
1. Hindmarsh, *John Newton and the Evangelical Tradition,* p.134.
2. As above.
3. As above, p.128.
4. As above, p.137.
5. See Jonah 4.
6. Quoted by Cecil, *John Newton,* p.163.

3. Spiritual disciplines
1. John Newton, *Cardiphonia,* 'Six Letters to the Rev. Mr B...', Letter 3.
2. Cecil, *John Newton,* p.193.
3. Brian Edwards, *Through Many Dangers,* Evangelical Press. Darlington, 2001, p.286.

4. The complete text of most of the hymns from which these extracts are taken is to be found elsewhere in the book.

5. Steve Turner, *Amazing Grace: The Story of America's Most Beloved Song*, Harper Collins, New York, p.137.

6. Hindmarsh, *John Newton and the Evangelical Tradition*, pp. 289-90.

4. Pastoral ministry

1. Cecil, *John Newton*, p.196.

2. As above, p.195.

3. As above, p.196.

4. Cecil, *John Newton*, p.110, quoting Scott's autobiography, *The Force of Truth*.

5. Quoted by Cecil, *John Newton*, p.181.

5. Hope beyond the grave

1. Edwards, *Through Many Dangers*, pp. 346-7.

Also available from the author

This CD contains fourteen of Newton's profound hymns set to
new music by Todd Murray.

Available online at www.beyondamazinggrace.com

or from:

Cardiphonia Productions
2509 Durwood Road
Little Rock
AR 72207
USA

Price: $15.00 (£10 sterling)